W9-CIL-360

THE CIGAR COMPANION

A Connoisseur's Guide

SECOND EDITION

ANTONIO Y CLEOPATRA
TOP QUALITY
BANCES
dunhill
VERY MILD
TAMPA FLA
CUESTA REY
CR
NATURAL
El Triunfo
Fabrica de Tabacos
LONG HAVANA FILLER
MARIA MANCINI
SANTA CLARA
1830
SAN ANDRES MEX.
CIFUENTES Y CIA
PARTAGAS
1845
Special Corona
TOPSTONE
SINCE 1903
FABRICA REG. 18
TE-AMO
MEXICO
21
TAMPA
HAV-A-TAMPA
CIGAR CORP.
RAMON ALLONES
1837
REG. U.S. PAT. OFF.
PRIMO DEL REY
HAND MADE
H. UPMANN
1844
MOCAMBO
MEXICO
MONTECRUZ
LA ROMANA
MONTESINO
BERING
DON PEPE
MEXICO
dunhill
CABAÑAS
MADE
TEMPLE HALL
JAMAICA
DUTCH MASTERS
THE MASTER CIGAR
ROMEO Y JULIETA
MEDALLAS DE ORO
DOMINICAN
IMPORTED
HAND MADE
HAND MADE
LA CORONA
HOYO DE MONTERREY
Canary
Quorum
Islands
CANARIA D'ORO
HAND MADE
VALLE DE SAN ANDRES
HAND
Pride of Jamaica
FLOR DE MEXICO
PERLA DEL MAR
HAVANO CIGAR CORP.
ROYAL JAMAICA
CIGARS
HAND MADE
CALIXTO LOPEZ
LORD BEACONSFIELD
Suerdieck Bahia
JOYA DE NICARAGUA
PUNCH
IMPORTED
HANDMADE
José Benito
A. FUENTE
Gran Reserva
TABACO
EL CAUDILLO
HAND MADE
LAS PALMAS

THE CIGAR COMPANION

A Connoisseur's Guide

SECOND EDITION

ANWER BATI & SIMON CHASE

MACMILLAN CANADA
Toronto

First published in Canada in 1995 by
Macmillan Canada

Canadian Cataloguing in Publication Data
Chase, Simon, 1944–
The Cigar Companion
Includes index.
ISBN 0-7715-7353-7
1. Cigars. I. Title.
TS2260.C37 1995 679'.72 C95-930776-1

The Cigar Companion was produced by
Quintet Publishing plc
The Old Brewery
6 Blundell Street
London N7 9BH

Senior Editor: Laura Sandelson
Creative Director: Richard Dewing
Designer: Ian Hunt
Project Editor: Anna Briffa
Editor: Susan Martineau
Photographers: Ian Howes & Paul Forrester

1 2 3 4 5 – 99 98 97 96 95

Typeset in Great Britain by
Central Southern Typesetters, Eastbourne
Manufactured in Singapore by
J. Film Process Pte Ltd
Printed in China by
Leefung-Asco Printers Ltd

CONTENTS

FOREWORD
– 6 –

INTRODUCTION
– 7 –

THE STORY OF CIGARS
– 8 –

THE CIGAR DIRECTORY
– 54 –

THE BUYING AND STORING OF CIGARS
– 213 –

CIGAR MERCHANT DIRECTORY
– 222 –

INDEX
– 224 –

AUTHOR ACKNOWLEDGEMENTS

It wouldn't have been possible to write this book without the help and support of a number of people in the cigar trade, so I would like to thank the following for the help they have given:

Carol Jean Llaneza of Villazon, Jan Verruso of the Consolidated Cigar Corporation, Robert Lillienfield of General Cigar, Lew Rothman and Jane Vargas of J.R. Tobacco, David Berkebile of Georgetown Tobacco in Washington, DC, Mr Guerlach of Forrestal, Edward Sahakian of the Davidoff shop in London, Kate Neill of Dunhill in London, Eva Bauernfeind of Davidoff in the United States, Graham Julius, Sergio Morera, Norman Buck, Paul Garmirian, Regla Jimenez of Habanos SA, Oscar Boruchin of Mike's Cigars, Joe Howe of Jack Schwartz Importers and George Brightman of *Cigar Aficionado*. And last but not least, editors: Stephen Paul, Laura Sandelson and Anna Briffa.

FOREWORD

It has been said that a fellow cigar smoker is a friend. I feel the same about cigar books.

My life is a story of passions, and one of my greatest moments is sitting back in a welcoming leather chair and carefully putting a match to an artfully-prepared, handrolled cigar. Each time I light up a great smoke from Cuba, the Dominican Republic, or Honduras, I take time to fully savor the complexity of the tobacco blend and the happy marriage between the filler tobacco, the binder leaf, and the silky-smooth wrapper.

I can see in my mind's eye the delicate, highly skilled fingers of an experienced roller applying the finishing touches to a cigar. As I remember the pungent aroma in a cigar factory, for a brief moment, everything else is blocked out from my mind. I recreate each step in the life of an outstanding cigar, from the deep emerald leaves in the field, to the sticky skin-smoothing humidity in a curing barn, to the carefully measured piles of tobacco on a rolling desk, and finally, to the deeply aromatic cedar aging rooms in which a cigar rests before beginning its journey.

One of my greatest moments with cigars was in Cuba. On my first trip to Havana, I was shown the Romeo Y Julieta factory. My visit was announced over a loudspeaker in the factory's main work room where 190 cigar rollers were busily rolling their daily quota of 100 cigars. On hearing I was an American journalist, they stopped, and in unison began banging their "chavettas" (cutting knives) on their desks. The rhythmic chorus of steel blades tapped on the hardened wood surfaces of the desks sent shivers up my spine. I was, literally, overcome with joy. I felt part of a worldwide network of cigar lovers.

I approach each smoke of a cigar with a sense of anticipation. Like many things in life, the more I know, the better understanding I have of it, and ultimately, emjoy it more. Well-researched books contribute greatly to my overall appreciation of a subject, and, with this book, my understanding of cigars will be greater and my pleasure undoubtedly enhanced.

MARVIN R. SHANKEN

MAY 1993

Marvin R. Shanken is the founder, editor, and publisher of *Cigar Aficionado* magazine, published quarterly since 1992. For information about subscriptions write to: Cigar Aficionado, 387 Park Avenue South, New York, New York 10016, Fax: 212–684–5424.

INTRODUCTION

The cigar has always had a very strong image in a way that the cigarette, despite its popularity, has never had. True, some cigarette brands evoke strong associations – the Marlboro cowboy, for instance – but only through advertising. Cigars, on the other hand, have acquired their image not only through the people who smoke them – one need only mention Winston Churchill, Edward VII, and any number of Hollywood film directors and producers such as Darryl F. Zanuck – but also through the occasions on which they are smoked. This applies to cigars in general, but handmade cigars, the subject of this book, in particular.

The aim of this book, whether you are a regular or occasional smoker of handmade cigars, is to tell you as much about them as possible and help you to understand the subject better. Above all, however, this book has been written to enhance your enjoyment of fine cigars and to encourage your interest in them.

ANWER BATI

MARCH 1993

My eighteen years in the cigar trade have been spent mainly in the company of Havanas. You should know that they pay my salary, so watch out in these pages for self-serving bias. Having said that, we are all biased by our own taste in cigars. Mine is unlikely to match yours and, in the end, the choice is personal.

Cigars have seen heady days since the first appearance of this book. The "Cigar Boom," "The Renaissance of the Cigar," call it what you will, started for me at Cuba's El Corojo plantation in February 1992. Anwer Bati, Marvin Shanken, and I stood watching the massive wrapper leaves inching their way to maturity under the muslin cover. Not even Marvin could have foreseen quite what was to follow.

In revising and updating *The Cigar Companion*, I hope to do justice to Anwer's original work and, like him, to augment the pleasure you obtain from your cigars.

SIMON CHASE

MAY 1995

1

THE STORY OF CIGARS

Nobody knows for sure *when* the tobacco plant was first cultivated, but there is little doubt about *where*. The native peoples of the American continent were undoubtedly the first not only to grow, but to smoke the plant, which probably first came from the Yucatán peninsula, Mexico. It was certainly used by the Maya of Central America, and when the Maya civilization was broken up, the scattered tribes carried tobacco both southward into South America, and to North America, where it was probably first used in the rites of the Mississippi Indians. It didn't come to the attention of the rest of the world until Christopher Columbus's momentous voyage of 1492.

Columbus himself was not particularly impressed by the custom, but soon Spanish and other European sailors fell for the habit, followed by the conquistadores and colonists. In due course the

THE AMERICAN INDIANS WERE ALMOST CERTAINLY THE FIRST PEOPLE TO SMOKE CIGARS.

LEFT: CHRISTOPHER COLUMBUS. HIS MEN WERE THE FIRST FROM EUROPE TO ENCOUNTER THE NORTH AMERICAN HABIT OF SMOKING.

returning conquistadores introduced tobacco smoking to Spain and Portugal. The habit, a sign of wealth, then spread to France, through the French ambassador to Portugal, Jean Nicot (who eventually gave his name to nicotine, and *Nicotiana tabacum*, the Latin name for tobacco), and to Italy. In Britain, as every schoolchild knows, Sir Walter Raleigh was probably responsible for introducing tobacco and the new fashion for smoking.

The word tobacco, some say, was a corruption of Tobago, the name of the Caribbean island. Others claim it comes from the Tabasco province of Mexico. Cohiba, a word used by the Taino Indians of Cuba was thought to mean tobacco, but now is considered to have referred to cigars. The word cigar originated from *sikar*, the Mayan word for smoking.

Although the first tobacco plantations were set up in Virginia in 1612, and Maryland in 1631, tobacco was smoked only in pipes in the American colonies. The cigar itself is thought not to have arrived until after 1762, when Israel Putnam, later an American general in the Revolutionary War, returned from Cuba, where he had been an officer in the British army. He came back to his home in Connecticut – an area where tobacco had been grown by settlers since the 17th century (and before them by the Indians) – with a selection of Havana cigars, and large amounts of Cuban tobacco. Before long, cigar factories were set up in the Hartford area, and the attempt was made to grow tobacco from Cuban seed. Production of the leaves started in the 1820s, and Connecticut tobacco today provides among the best wrapper leaves to be found outside Cuba. By the early 19th century, not only were Cuban cigars being imported into the United States, but domestic production was also taking off.

The habit of smoking cigars (as opposed to using tobacco in other forms) spread out to the rest of Europe from Spain where cigars, using Cuban tobacco, were made in Seville from 1717 onward. By 1790, cigar manufacture had spread north of the Pyrenees, with small factories being set up in France and Germany. But cigar smoking didn't really take off in France and Britain until after the Peninsular War (1806–12) against Napoleon, when returning British and French veterans spread the habit they had learned while serving in Spain. By this time the pipe had been replaced by snuff as the main way of taking tobacco, and cigars now became the fashionable way of smoking it. Production of segars, as they were known, began in Britain in 1820, and in 1821 an Act of Parliament was needed to set out regulations governing production. Because of a

FERDINAND VII KING OF SPAIN. HE VIGOROUSLY PROMOTED THE PRODUCTION OF CUBAN CIGARS.

new import tax, foreign cigars in Britain were already regarded as a luxury item.

Soon there was a demand for higher-quality cigars in Europe, and the Sevillas, as Spanish cigars were called, were superseded by those from Cuba (then a Spanish colony), not least as the result of a decree by King Ferdinand VII of Spain in 1821, encouraging the production of Cuban cigars, a Spanish state monopoly. Cigar smoking became such a widespread custom in Britain and France that smoking cars became a feature of European trains, and the smoking room was introduced in clubs and hotels. The habit even influenced clothing – with the introduction of the smoking jacket. In France, tuxedos are still referred to as *le smoking.* By the end of the 19th century, the after-dinner cigar, with port or brandy, was a firmly established tradition. It was given an added boost by the fact that the Prince of Wales (the future Edward VII), a leader of fashion, was a devotee, much to the chagrin of his mother, Queen Victoria, who was not amused by the habit.

Cigar smoking didn't really take off in the United States until the time of the Civil War (although John Quincy Adams, 6th President of the United States, was a confirmed cigar smoker at the beginning of the century; later, President Ulysses Grant was also to become a devotee) with the most expensive domestic cigars,

ILLUSTRATION OF A MID-19TH-CENTURY CIGAR FACTORY IN ENGLAND.

made with Cuban tobacco, called clear Havanas. The name Havana, by now, had become a generic term. Some of the best-known domestic cigars came from the factory at Conestoga, Pennsylvania, where the long "stogie" cigar was made. By the late 19th century, the cigar had become a status symbol in the United States, and branding became important. Thus, there was Henry Clay, for instance, named after the Senator. A tax reduction in the 1870s made the cigar even more popular and widely available, and encouraged domestic production. By 1919, Thomas Marshall, Woodrow Wilson's Vice President was able to say in the Senate: "What this country really needs is a good five-cent cigar," an ambition not to be achieved until almost 40 years later when new methods of cigar production allowed truly cheap cigars to be made by machine. Cigar sales in the United States have, however, declined over the last 20 years – from 9 billion cigars (of all types) in 1970, to 2 billion today.

Machine production of cigars wasn't introduced until the 1920s (in Cuba, the Por Larranaga firm was the first to attempt it, and handmade production in the United States fell from 90 percent in 1924, to a mere 2 percent by the end of the 1950s.

It was a different story in Cuba, where the cigar became a national symbol. Cuban peasants started becoming *vegueros*, tobacco growers, from the 16th century onward, waging a constant

NOTE THE WOMEN SMOKING CIGARS AS THEY LEAVE A CIGAR FACTORY IN MANILA.

battle against big landowners as exports of the crop grew. Some of them became tenant farmers or sharecroppers; others were forced to find new land to farm, opening up areas such as Pinar del Rio and Oriente.

By the mid-19th century, by which time there was free trade in tobacco, there were 9,500 plantations, and factories in Havana and other cities sprang up (at one stage, there were as many as 1,300, though there were only around 120 by the beginning of the 20th century), and cigar production became a fully fledged industry. Export was mainly to the United States until tariff barriers were put up in 1857. During the same period, brand and size differentiation began, and the cigar box and band were introduced.

As the industry grew, the cigar makers became the core of the Cuban industrial working class, and a unique institution was set up in 1865, which lasts to this day: the reading of literary, political, and other texts, including the works of Zola, Dumas, and Victor Hugo, to the rollers by fellow workers. This was to alleviate the boredom, and help the cause of worker education. During the last quarter of the 19th century, faced with the growing political upheaval caused by the struggle for independence from Spain, many cigar makers emigrated to the United States or nearby islands like Jamaica, where they set up cigar industries in towns like Tampa, Key West, and Kingston.

SUPERLATIVE CUBAN CIGARS ARE STILL MADE EXCLUSIVELY FOR FIDEL CASTRO, THE CUBAN LEADER, TO PRESENT TO STATE VISITORS AND DIPLOMATS.

These Cubans abroad were instrumental in funding the revolt against Spain, led in 1895 by José Martí, the Cuban national hero, and later the increasingly politicized cigar workers in Cuba were to take an important part in national life. Martí's order for the uprising was, symbolically, sent from Key West to Cuba inside a cigar. Cigar workers continued at the center of political consciousness after Fidel Castro's revolution against General Batista in 1959. After Castro started to nationalize Cuban and foreign assets, the United States embargo on Cuba, imposed in 1962, meant that Havana cigars could no longer be legally imported into the United States, except in small quantities for personal use. The cigar industry – much of which had been American-owned – was nationalized along with everything else and put under the control of the state monopoly, Cubatabaco.

Many of the dispossessed cigar factory owners such as the Palicio, Cifuentes, and Menendez families fled abroad, determined to start production up again, often using the same brand names they had owned in Cuba. As a result, cigars called Romeo Y Julieta, H. Upmann, and Partagas are made in the Dominican Republic; La Gloria Cubana in Miami; Punch and Hoyo de Monterrey in Honduras; and Sancho Panza in Mexico. In the case of Montecruz cigars, the name was slightly changed from the original Montecristo, and they were originally made in the Canary Islands, though they are now manufactured in the Dominican Republic. These brands using Cuban names usually bear no relation in terms of flavor to their Havana counterparts, however well made they may be. Entirely new brands, too, such as Don Miguel, Don Diego, and Montesino were also set up. After two decades of investment by both local and American companies, the Dominican Republic has seen rapid growth in its cigar industry during the 1990s. More than any other country, it has benefitted from the explosion of American consumer enthusiasm for handmade cigars touched off by the launch of *Cigar Aficionado* magazine in September 1992.

At the start of the decade, sales from the Dominican Republic to the United States had been expanding at a rate of around 5 percent per year. This leapt to 18 percent in 1993 when 55 million handmade cigars were shipped, accounting for just over half of all the handmade cigars imported into the United States. In 1994 growth continued, adding another 20 percent overall, with some factories claiming increases of nearly 40 percent. The greatest problem facing the Dominican Republican manufacturers today appears to be finding enough tobaccos of quality for handmade cigars.

The early 1990s have been less kind to Cuba. In the two years following the collapse of the Soviet Union, half of the island's gross domestic product evaporated. The cigar industry suffered less than most because its essential raw material – tobacco – is all grown on the island. Nonetheless, shortages of fertilizers, packaging materials, and even such mundane items as string, all of which had come from the former Eastern bloc, took their toll.

The weather played its part, too. Unseasonal rains in the Vuelta Abajo constrained the 1991 and 1992 harvests. Then the great storm of March 1993, which ended up depositing ten feet of snow on New York City, started life wreaking havoc in the Partido wrapper-growing region. Production of Havanas, which had topped 80 million in 1990, fell to around 50 million by 1994. If cigar enthusiasts around the world have been forced to search hard for their preferred Havana, their difficulties pale into insignificance alongside the trials of their Cuban counterparts. Domestic cigar production tumbled by well over half from a remarkable figure of 280 million in 1990, and stringent rationing was introduced.

Such changes of fortune are nothing new to Cuba's hardy population. Just after the revolution, cigar exports dropped to 30 million.

THE ARCHETYPAL VIEW OF THE CIGAR SMOKER: GOOD WINE, GOOD TOBACCO.

Habanos SA, the company which recently took over most of the marketing responsibilities for Havanas from the state-owned Cubatabaco, has arranged hard currency deals with its international partners to supply materials for the crops from 1995 onward.

There can be few symbols of capitalism and plutocracy more potent than the cigar. Tycoons rarely seem happier, or more prosperous, than when pictured puffing a large Havana. It says: power, privilege, prestige – and, above all, expense. But the irony, of course, is that Havana cigars are produced in one of the world's few remaining bastions of communism.

It would be quite wrong to give the impression that the growing of cigar tobacco and the production of cigars is limited to Cuba and the Dominican Republic. Nearby Jamaica has had its own industry for over a century, and several Central American countries like Mexico, Honduras, and Nicaragua enjoy traditions of cigar making that go back much further. Ecuador now produces a good-quality wrapper, oddly known as Ecuador/Connecticut, and Brazil brings its own unique flavor and style to the creation of cigars. Further afield, the Indonesian islands of Java and Sumatra have time-honored links with the cigar makers of the Netherlands, Germany, and Switzerland, as do the Philippines with Spain. Africa's contribution comes from Cameroon, in the form of some of the most sought-after, rich, dark wrappers in the world.

THE DOMINICAN REPUBLIC

The Dominican Republic, east of Cuba, has a similar climate and very good tobacco-growing conditions, particularly in the Cibao River valley. It has, over the last 15 years or so, become a major exporter of top quality handmade cigars, particularly to the United States, which imports around 60 million cigars a year from there. This accounts for half of the American handmade cigar market. It has attracted major cigar manufacturers such as General Cigar (with brands like Canario D'Oro and Partagas) and Consolidated Cigar (brand names such as Don Diego and Primo del Rey). Consolidated moved its operations to the Dominican Republic from the Canary Islands. Most of the tobacco grown in the Dominican Republic is for fillers only. Virtually all the wrappers and many of the binders for cigars made there are imported from countries like the U.S. (Connecticut), Cameroon (for Partagas, for instance), Brazil, Honduras, Mexico, and Ecuador. Some fillers, too, are brought in from abroad. Major efforts, led by the Fuente family, are now being made to extend the variety of tobaccos grown in the country. Even wrappers, always the toughest challenge, are now to be seen on the Fuente's plantations . . . and on some of their cigars.

CONNECTICUT VALLEY

The sandy loam of the Connecticut valley (where conditions suitable for growing top-quality cigar tobacco are created under huge, 10-foot high tents), and the use of the Hazelwood strain of Cuban seed produces some of the world's best wrapper leaves, called Connecticut Shade. The leaves are very expensive to produce and sell for as much as $40 a pound, adding between 50 cents and a dollar to the price of a cigar. The growing cycle begins in March, with the harvest taking place in August. The drying process, though essentially the same as in Cuba, is helped, in Connecticut, by the use of careful heating from below using gas burners. Connecticut wrappers are used for cigars such as Macanudo, and the Dominican-made Davidoffs.

PINAR DEL RIO *an*

There are those who disagree (the leaf producers of Connecticut, the Dominican Republic, and Honduras foremost among them), but it is still generally acknowledged that the finest cigar tobacco in the world comes from Cuba, and in particular from the Vuelta Abajo area of the Pinar del Rio province.

Pinar del Rio is the region at the western end of Cuba, situated between mountains and the coast, the island's third largest province. The area, which points toward the Mexican Yucatán peninsula, is undulating, green, and lush (it was under the sea in prehistoric times), rather resembling southeast Asia or parts of southern Louisiana and Florida. Life and living conditions there are primitive for the 600,000 inhabitants, with none of the sophistication or development to be found near Havana. But the agricultural conditions – climate, rainfall, and soil (a reddish sandy loam) – are perfect for tobacco production, by far the main industry. Tobacco is grown on smallholdings (many of them privately owned, but selling tobacco to the government at a fixed

price), totaling about 100,000 acres. They create a patchwork effect across the plains. Before the revolution, large tracts of land were owned by the main tobacco companies, but today, although vegueros can own up to 150 acres, most cultivate from five to ten acres. Outside the tobacco season, maize is often grown on the same land. Vuelta Abajo takes up most of the 160 square miles of Pinar del Rio. Tobacco grows freely here, but the finest, destined

VUELTA ABAJO, CUBA

for cigars to be known as Havanas or Habanos, comes from a surprisingly small area centered around the two towns of San Juan y Martinez and San Luis. Not much more than 2,500 acres are devoted to wrappers and 5,000 acres to fillers and binders. Amongst the best known plantations are El Corojo, where the Corojo wrapper plant was developed, and Hoyo de Monterrey, famous for its fillers.

The rainfall in Pinar del Rio is among the highest in Cuba, with 65 inches a year, although significant for tobacco growth, only 8 inches or so of rain – over an average of 26 days – falls during the main growing months from November to February. They come in the middle of La Seca, the dry season, by which time the soil has had plenty of rain from storms in the period from May to October. Temperatures during the growing season reach average highs of 80°F, with around 8 hours a day of sunshine, and average humidity of 64 percent. The Semivuelta area is the second tobacco-growing area of Pinar del Rio, and produces thicker leaves, with a stronger aroma than those of Vuelta Abajo. This tobacco was once exported to the United States, but is now used for the domestic cigar industry.

The Partido area, near Havana, also grows high-quality wrappers for handmade Havanas. Remedios in the island's center, and Oriente at its eastern end produce tobacco, too, but not for top-quality cigars.

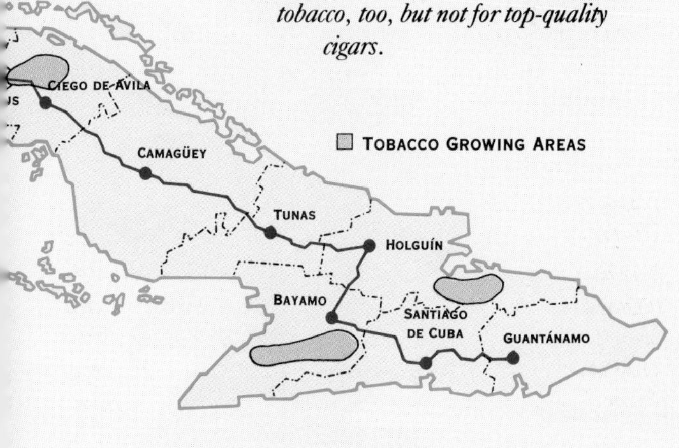

GROWING CIGAR TOBACCO

The following passage is specifically for Havana cigars, but the process is, broadly speaking, similar elsewhere.

Cigars are a natural product, often compared to wine (though the comparison sometimes tends to get out of hand), and the quality of a cigar is directly related to the type and quality of leaves used in its construction, just as the quality of wine depends on the type and quality of grapes used.

Tobacco seedbeds have to be in flat fields, so that the seeds aren't washed away. After being planted, the seeds are covered with cloth or straw to shade them from the sun. This covering is gradually removed as they begin to germinate, and after around 35 days (during which the seed will be sprayed with pesticides), they are transplanted – usually in the second half of October – into the tobacco fields proper. The leaves are watered both by rain and the morning dew, and irrigated from below.

The tobacco plant is considered in three parts: the top, or corona, the middle, and the bottom. As the leaves develop, buds appear. These have to be removed by hand to prevent them from stunting leaf and plant growth. The quality of wrapper leaf is crucial in any

CUBAN TOBACCO PLANT

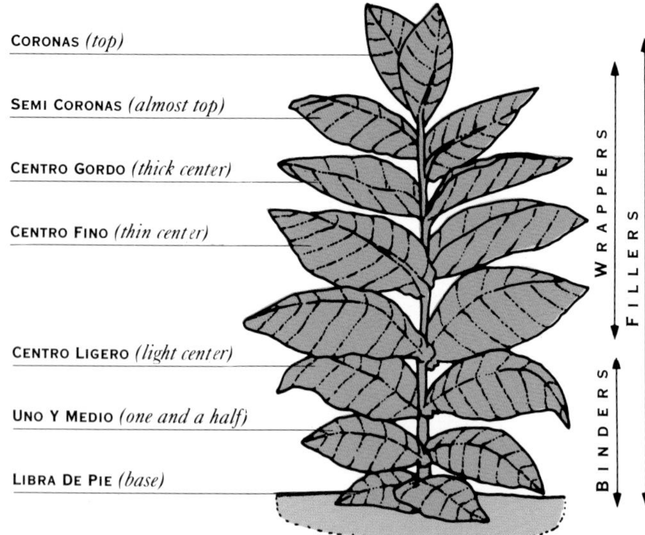

cigar. Plants called Corojos, specifically designated to provide wrapper leaves for the very best cigars, are always grown under gauze sheets held up by tall wooden poles. They prevent the leaves from becoming too thick in a protective response to sunlight. The technique, called *tapado* (covering), also helps them to remain smooth.

When harvesting time arrives, leaves are removed by hand, using a single movement. Those selected as wrappers are put in bundles of five, a manojo, or hand. The leaves are picked in six phases: *libra de pie* (at the base), *uno y medio* (one-and-a-half), *centro ligero* (light cente), *centro fino* (thin center), *centro gordo* (thick center), and *corona* (crown). The *libra de pie* section isn't used for wrappers. A week passes between each phase. The finest leaves found in the middle of the plant; the top leaves *(corona)* are usually too oily to be used for wrappers, except for domestic consumption, and are often used as binder leaves. The whole cycle, from transplanted seedlings to the end of harvesting takes some 120 days, with each plant being visited an average of 170 times – making it a very labor-intensive process.

Wrapper leaves grown under cover are classified by color as *ligero* (light), *seco* (dry), *viso* (glossy), *amarillo* (yellow), *medio tiempo* (half texture), and *quebrado* (broken), while those grown under the sun are divided into *volado*, *seco*, *ligero*, and *medio tiempo*. The ligero leaves from the top of the plant have a very strong flavor, the seco

EL COROJO WRAPPER PLANTATION IN SAN LUÌS ONE WEEK AFTER PLANTING.

Harvested wrapper leaves arrive at curing barn, La Guira, Cuba.

from the middle are much lighter, and the volado leaves from the bottom are used to add bulk and for their burning qualities. The art of making a good cigar is to blend these, along with a suitable wrapper leaf, in such proportions as to give the eventual cigar a mild, medium, or full flavor, and to ensure that it burns well. The leaves are also classified by size (large, average, small) and by physical condition (unhealthy or broken leaves are used for cigarettes or machine-made cigars). If all the leaves are good, each wrapper plant can wrap 32 cigars. The condition and quality of the wrapper leaf is crucial to the attractive appearance of a cigar, as well as its aroma.

The bundles of leaves are then taken to a tobacco barn on the *vega*, or plantation, to be cured. The barns face west so that the sun heats one end in the morning, and the other in the late afternoon. The temperature and humidity in the barns is carefully controlled, if necessary by opening and closing the doors at both ends (usually kept shut) to take account of changes of temperature or rainfall.

Once the leaves reach the barn, they are strung up on poles, or *cujes*, using needle and thread. The poles, each holding around 100 leaves, are hoisted up horizontally (their position high in the barn allows air to circulate), and the leaves left to dry for between 45 and 60 days, depending on the weather. During this time, the green chlorophyll in the leaves turns to brown carotene, giving them their characteristic color. The poles are then taken down, the threads cut, and the leaves stacked into bundles according to type.

The bundles are then taken to the fermentation houses and placed in piles about three feet high, covered with jute. Enough moisture remains in the leaves to spark the first fermentation, a process like composting. Heat develops, but the temperature must be watched carefully so that it does not exceed 92°F during the 35 to 40 days that the piles are left intact. The leaves assume a uniform color.

The piles are then broken up and the leaves cooled. The next stop in their journey is at the *escogida*, or sorting house, where they will be graded according to color, size, and texture and where the fillers will have part of their stems stripped out. In preparation for handling, they are moistened either under a spray of pure water for wrappers or a mixture of water and the juices from tobacco stems for fillers.

THREADING THE WRAPPER LEAVES TOGETHER. THEY ARE HUNG UP IN BATCHES OF 50.

CIGAR TOBACCO PRODUCTION

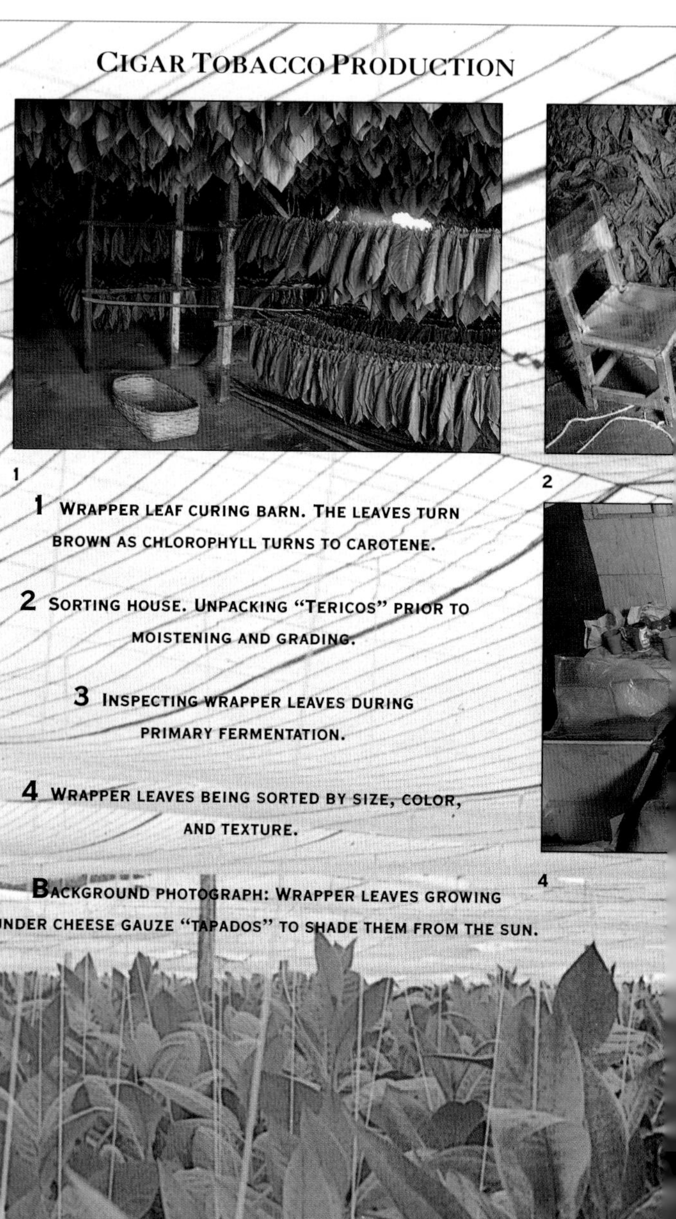

1 2 4

1 WRAPPER LEAF CURING BARN. THE LEAVES TURN BROWN AS CHLOROPHYLL TURNS TO CAROTENE.

2 SORTING HOUSE. UNPACKING "TERICOS" PRIOR TO MOISTENING AND GRADING.

3 INSPECTING WRAPPER LEAVES DURING PRIMARY FERMENTATION.

4 WRAPPER LEAVES BEING SORTED BY SIZE, COLOR, AND TEXTURE.

BACKGROUND PHOTOGRAPH: WRAPPER LEAVES GROWING UNDER CHEESE GAUZE "TAPADOS" TO SHADE THEM FROM THE SUN.

3

Traditionally, women perform the tasks of sorting and stripping. Each leaf is tenderly examined and graded. Broken leaves are set aside for use in cigarettes.

Flattened onto boards *(planchas)*, the leaves return to the fermentation area. In dark rooms, they are built into stacks called *burros* up to 6 feet high. The second, more powerful fermentation begins within the damp leaves. A perforated wooden casing has been buried in the *burro*, into which a sword-like thermometer is thrust. The temperature inside must not exceed 110°F for around 60 days, longer for some leaf types, shorter for others. If it does, the bulk is broken down and the leaves cooled before it is rebuilt. Ammonia is released as the leaves shed their impurities.

Because of the fermentation process, cigar tobacco is much lower in acidity, tar, and nicotine than cigarette tobacco, making it much more palatable.

It is now time for the leaves to be sent to the factories or warehouses in *tercios*, square bales wrapped with palm bark, which help to keep the tobacco at a constant humidity, and slowly mature until it is needed – sometimes for as long as two years.

These long and complicated processes of selection and fermentation have to be carefully supervised and are crucial to the final flavor of handmade cigars.

WRAPPER LEAVES FOR COHIBA CIGARS MOISTENED BEFORE GOING TO CIGAR ROLLER.

THE STRUCTURE OF A CIGAR

Handmade cigars have three constituent parts – the filler, the binder, and the wrapper. Each of the parts has a different function when the cigar is actually smoked.

The outside wrapper (or *capa*) dictates the cigar's appearance. As described, it is always grown under gauze and fermented separately from other leaves to ensure that it is smooth, not too oily, and has a subtle bouquet. It also has to be soft and pliable so that it is easy for the roller to handle.

Wrapper leaves from different plantations have varying colors (and thus subtly different flavors, more sugary if they are darker, for instance) and are used for different brands. Good wrapper leaves have to be elastic and must have no protruding veins. They have to be matured for between one year and 18 months, the longer the better. Wrappers of handmade non-Cuban cigars might come from Connecticut, Cameroon, Sumatra, Ecuador, Honduras, Mexico, Costa Rica, or Nicaragua. The wrapper is the most expensive part of the cigar.

The binder leaf (capote) holds the cigar together and is usually two halves of coarse sun-grown leaf from the upper part of the plant, chosen because of its good tensile strength.

The filler is made of separate leaves folded by hand along their length, to allow a passage through which smoke can be drawn when the cigar is lit. The fold can only be properly achieved by hand and is the primary reason why machine-made cigars are less satisfactory. This style of arranging the filler is sometimes called the "book" style – which means that if you were to cut the cigar down its length with a razor, the filler leaves would resemble the pages of a book. In the past, the filler was sometimes arranged using the "entubar" method – with up to eight narrow tubes of tobacco leaf rolled into the binder – making the cigar very slow-burning.

Three different types of leaf are normally used for the filler (in fatter sizes, like Montecristo No. 2, a fourth type is also used).

Ligero leaves from the top of the plant are dark and full in flavor as a result of oils produced by exposure to sunlight. They have to be matured for at least two years before they can be used in cigar making. Ligero tobacco is always placed in the middle of the cigar, because it burns slowly.

Seco leaves, from the middle of the plant, are much lighter in color and flavor. They are usually used after maturing for around 18 months.

Volado leaves, from the bottom of the plant, have little or no flavor, but they have good burning qualities. They are matured for about nine months before use.

The precise blend of these different leaves in the filler dictates the flavor of each brand and size. A full-bodied cigar like Ramon Allones will, for instance, have a higher proportion of ligero in its filler, than a mild cigar such as H. Upmann, where seco and volado will predominate. Small, thin cigars will very often have no ligero leaf in them at all. The consistency of a blend is achieved by using tobacco from different harvests and farms, so a large stock of matured tobacco is essential to the process.

ROLLING A CIGAR

In making a handmade cigar, two to four filler leaves (depending on the size and strength of the cigar) are laid end to end and rolled into the two halves of the binder leaves – making up what is called the "bunch." Great skill is required to make sure that the filler is evenly distributed so that the cigar will draw properly. Wooden molds are used into which the filler blend (rolled into the binder) is pressed by the "bunchers," with a mechanical press then used to complete the process. In the Havana factory, the bunching is done by the same person who eventually adds the wrapper. The practice is slightly different in, for instance, the factories of the Dominican Republic, where specialist bunchers work in teams with specialist wrapper rollers. In both systems, the result is that each roller has a supply of ready molded fillers, prepared for what is being made on that day, at his or her work bench.

GATHERING THE BLEND OF FILLER LEAVES.

ROLLING A CIGAR

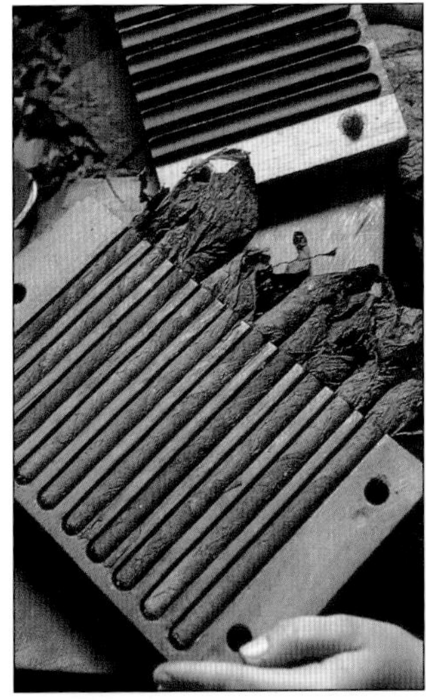

ROLLING COHIBA LANCERO CIGARS AT EL LAGUITO FACTORY, HAVANA.

AFTER PRESSING, THE "BUNCHES" ARE READY TO HAVE WRAPPER LEAVES ROLLED AROUND THEM.

THE "CHAVETA" IS USED TO TRIM SURPLUS TOBACCO.

THE FRAGILE WRAPPER IS GENTLY STRETCHED BEFORE ROLLING.

Surplus filler is trimmed from the end to form a round top. A wrapper leaf is then selected, the remaining stalk is stripped off the binder, and the wrapper is trimmed to the right size (using the central part of the leaf, placed upside-down, to avoid having any veins showing) with an oval steel blade called a chaveta. The cylinder of tobacco in its binder (the "bunch") is now laid at an angle across the wrapper, which is then stretched as necessary and wound carefully around the binder, overlapping at each turn, until it is stuck down using a tiny drop of colorless and flavorless tragacanth vegetable gum. The cigar is then rolled, applying gentle pressure, with the flat part of the steel blade to make sure its construction is even. Next, a small round piece of wrapper (about the size of a small coin) is cut out from the trimmings on hand to form the cap, which is stuck in place. In the case of cigars such as the Montecristo Especial, the closed end is sealed by twisting the end of the wrapper. This is a version of what is known as the "flag" method of capping a cigar – a highly skilled process in which the wrapper itself is smoothed down to form the cap. The flag method is only used on the best handmade cigars, and never on machine-mades. Finally, the open end is guillotined to the correct length.

The construction of a cigar is a crucial factor in how well you enjoy it. If it is under-filled, it will draw easily, but burn fast, and get hot and harsh as a result. If it is over-filled, it will be difficult to draw on, or "plugged." Good cigars have to be consistent. That relies on skill, quality control, and the resources (reserves of suitable leaf, essentially) to guarantee that this year's cigars are the same as last year's, even if there is a bad harvest.

FITTING THE CAP

A SEPARATE PIECE OF WRAPPER IS USUALLY USED TO CAP THE CIGAR.

THE LEGENDARY PARTAGAS FACTORY, HAVANA.

THE HAVANA CIGAR FACTORY

The Havana cigar factory today is much as it was when the art of cigar making was standardized in the mid-19th century and the production of cigars became industrialized. There are only eight factories making handmade cigars in Cuba today (compared with 120 at the beginning of the century). The names of the factories were all officially changed after the revolution to what were considered more ideologically sound titles, but most of them are still commonly referred to by their pre-revolutionary names, and still display their old signs outside. The best known are H. Upmann (now called José Marti), Partagas (Francisco Perez German), Romeo Y Julieta (Briones Montoto), La Corona (Fernando Roig), and the elite El Laguito, which originally opened in the mid-1960s as a training school. Each factory specializes in a number of brands of a particular flavor. The Partagas factory, for instance, specializes in full-bodied cigars, producing six brands including Bolivar, Ramon Allones, Gloria Cubana and, of course, Partagas. Factories also often specialize in making a particular range of sizes.

The procedures in the various factories are essentially the same, though the size and atmosphere of each factory differs. The grand El Laguito, for instance, is an Italianate mansion (built in 1910) and former home of the Marquez de Pinar del Rio. It is located in three buildings in a swanky residential suburb. The rather gloomy three-story Partagas factory, on the other hand, which was built in downtown Havana in 1845, is rather more down to earth. Laguito was the first factory to use female rollers, and even today the majority of the 94 rollers there are women. The 200 rollers at the

THE MANUFACTURING PROCESS OF HAVANA CIGARS

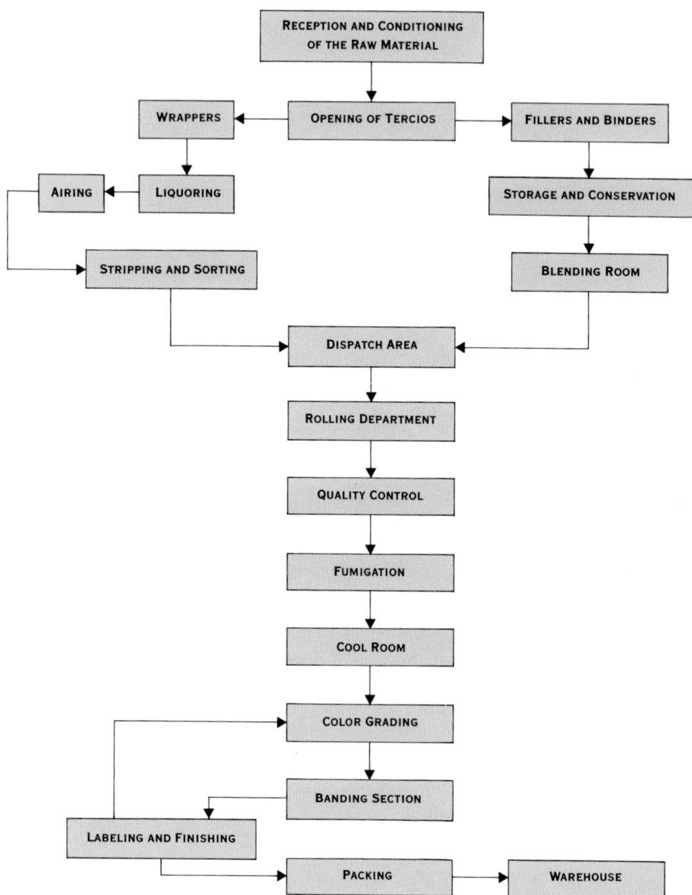

Partagas factory, the biggest for export production, turn out 5 million cigars a year. No matter which factory you go to, the walls of all of them display revolutionary slogans and portraits of Castro, Che Guevara, and others. Other slogans announce "La calidad es el respeto al pueblo" (Quality is respect for people) or "Tu tambien haces calidad" (You have to care about quality).

It has been estimated that a handmade Havana cigar goes through no fewer than 222 different stages from seedling to the finished product, before being ready for distribution. And the care and expertise shown at the factory is not only crucial to the final

Cigar roller, Havana.

appearance of the cigar, but also affects how well it burns and what it actually tastes like. Not surprisingly, apprenticeship for the task of roller is a lengthy and competitive process, taking nine months. Even then, many fail, and those who succeed are confined to making small-sized cigars before being allowed to graduate to the larger, generally fuller-flavored, sizes.

The cigar rollers, or *torcedores*, work in large rooms where the old custom, dating from 1864, of reading aloud from books and newspapers continues to this day. The radio is also switched on, from time to time, to bring the news and important announcements. The worker who acts as reader (lector), selected by his peers for his expressive voice and literacy, is compensated by a small payment from each of the rollers, all of whom are paid piece work, according to the number of cigars they produce. Each roller is

TYPICAL WORKPLACE OF A CIGAR ROLLER.

responsible for seeing a cigar through from the bunching stage until it is finally trimmed to size. The ready-blended combination of filler leaves and binder are prepared in advance by each roller and pressed in wooden molds of the appropriate size. The use of molds started in around 1958, before the Cuban revolution. As a result, the cigar rollers – sitting at benches rather like old-fashioned school desks – each start with a quota of filler appropriate to the size and brand of cigar being made that day. All is concentration: errors are costly. But the atmosphere is cheerful, the torcedores taking great pride in their work. If a visitor enters the room, the rollers greet him by tapping their chavetas in unison on their tables.

There are as many as 42 handmade cigar sizes made today, and a good cigar maker can usually roll around 120 medium-sized cigars (though exceptionally skilled rollers can make as many as 150) a day – an average of four to five minutes for a cigar. But the average for the Montecristo A size is only 56 cigars a day. Some star rollers, such as Jesus Ortiz at the H. Upmann factory, can do much better: he can produce a staggering 200 Montecristo As a day.

The torcedores work an eight-hour day, usually six days a week, for around 350–400 pesos ($350–400 at the official exchange rate) a month. They are allowed to take home five cigars a day and can smoke as many as they wish while they work.

There are seven grades of worker in the Havana factory, the least experienced rollers (in grade 4) making only cigars up to and including the petit corona size; those in grade 5 making corona size and above, and those in grades 6 and 7 (the latter consists of a handful of star rollers) making the difficult specialist sizes such as

QUALITY CONTROL

QUALITY CONTROL. CHECKING THE GIRTH AND LENGTH OF A COHIBA LANCERO.

MIRIAM LOPEZ, EL LAGUITO'S ONLY FEMALE TASTER, ASSESSES A COHIBA LANCERO.

pyramides. The skill of the roller is reflected in the eventual cost per inch of the cigar. The smaller sizes are, in other words, cheaper than the larger ones.

Using colored ribbon, each roller ties his or her cigars into bundles (all of the same size and brand) of 50. Most of these bundles (*media ruedas*, or "half wheels") go into a vacuum fumigation chamber, where the cigars are treated against potential pests. A proportion of each roller's output is also taken to be checked for quality.

The man in charge of quality control at El Laguito, Fernando Valdez, tests a fifth of each roller's daily output (though only 10 percent of cigars are checked at the Partagas factory) according to no fewer than eight different criteria such as length, weight, firmness, smoothness of the wrappers, and whether or not the ends are well cut. Later, cigars from different batches are actually blind tasted by a team of six catadores, or professional smokers – themselves rigorously examined every six months – who must assess qualities such as a cigar's aroma, how well it burns, and how easily it draws. The importance of each category varies according to the type of cigar. When testing a fat robusto, for instance, the flavor is paramount, but in the slim panatela size, draw is more important. There is a standard for each type of cigar. The catadores do their tasting in the morning only, smoking about an inch of each cigar, and refreshing their palates with sugarless tea. By the end of any given week, every roller's work will have been tasted.

After being removed from the vacuum chamber, cigars are held in special cool cabinets (*escaparates*) for three weeks, in order to shed any excess moisture acquired in the factory and settle down any fermentation that is taking place. A cabinet might hold up to 18,000 cigars, all kept under careful supervision.

When they are ready, batches of 1,000 cigars from a particular brand and size are sent in wooden boxes to be graded according to appearance. The cigars are classified into as many as 65 different shades – and each selector must be familiar with all of them. First the selector takes into account the basic color of the cigar (hues given names such as sangre de toro, encendido, colorado encendido, colorado, colorado pajizo, and clarisimo), and then the shade within that particular color category. The color grader then puts the cigars into transit boxes, making sure that all the cigars in a particular box are the same color. The darkest cigar is placed on the left of the box, and the cigars arranged according to nuances of shade so that the lightest is on the right.

FINISHING AND PACKAGING

CIGARS SORTED INTO DIFFERENT COLOR SHADES.

THE BAND IS ADDED.

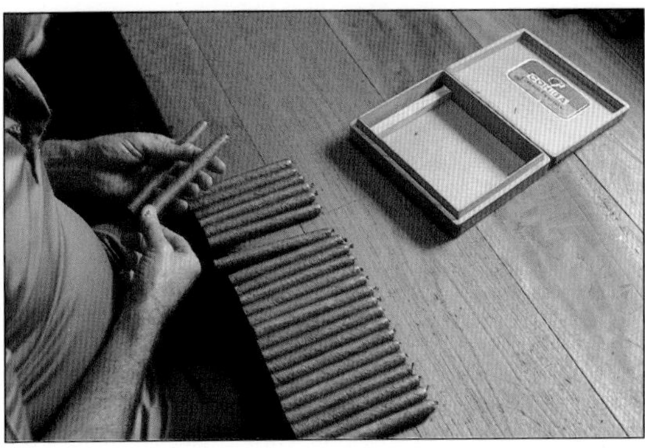

CIGARS ARE BOXED ACCORDING TO COLOR.

Once the cigars are color-graded, they go to the packing department, where bands are put on. The cigars are then put in the familiar cedar boxes in which they will be sold. The packers also watch out for cigars which have escaped the quality control department. Once the final box is filled, the cigars are checked again, and then a thin leaf of cedar wood is laid on top of them.

The box is then sealed with the essential label guaranteeing that it is a genuine box of Havanas or Habanos. The word "Habanos" in red on a chevron has been added to boxes since 1994.

The practice of making handmade cigars is essentially the same wherever they're made, but in the Dominican Republic, for instance, the arrangement between bunchers and rollers is sometimes different (the jobs usually being separated). The large, modern American-owned factories of the Dominican Republic have state-of-the-art quality-control methods, using machines (at the bunch stage, as well as later) to check suction, and thus how well a cigar will draw. Despite this, other manufacturers still prefer to do everything by hand, particularly checking for gaps in the bunch, which will make a cigar overheat. In the Philippines, there is a method of rolling in which leaves are spiraled around two thin wooden sticks, which are removed when the cigar is wrapped.

HANDMADE VERSUS MACHINE-MADE CIGARS

The essential difference between handmade and machine-made cigars lies in the fact that, on the whole, most machine-made cigars aren't made with long fillers – fillers, that is, which run the whole length of the cigar – thus making the drawing and burning qualities (they burn faster and become hotter) of the machine-mades significantly inferior. Some machine-made brands, Bering for instance, use long fillers, making them better but still inferior to handmade cigars. The quality of wrappers on machine-made cigars is also usually inferior to those used on the best handmades.

For cheap, mass market, machine-made brands, blended filler is fed into rod-making machines – a process similar to cigarette making – and covered by a continuous sheet of binder. This creates a tube which is sealed at each end to the appropriate length. The wrapper is then added and the cigars trimmed.

In the case of more expensive machine-mades, an operator sitting in front of a cigar-making machine feeds a mixture of filler tobacco (usually shredded leaves or scraps) into a hopper, and places two

THE DIFFERENCE BETWEEN CIGAR TYPES

MACHINE-MADE: THE FILLER IS MADE OF SCRAPS OF LEAF.

HANDMADE: FILLER, BINDER, WRAPPER. NOTE THE LONG FILLER WHICH RUNS THE LENGTH OF THE CIGAR.

binder leaves on a plate where they are cut. The two leaves are then positioned, overlapping, on a moving belt which feeds them into the rolling machine. This wraps the measured amount of filler and feeds out the cigar, which is then trimmed.

It is reasonably easy to tell the difference between handmade cigars and all but the best machine-mades: the caps on machine-mades are often very much more pointed; the cigars tend to be much less smooth to the touch; and the wrapper is likely to be much coarser, quite often with protruding veins. If a cigar doesn't have a cap, you can be certain that it is one of the cheaper machine-mades. Cellophane wrapping can also be a giveaway, particularly with Cuban cigars, but many very good non-Cuban handmade brands come wrapped in cellophane, so this is by no means an infallible way of telling whether the cigars are machine-made or not.

The Cubans recently introduced the concept of "hand-finished" machine-bunched cigars, with the Quintero brand for instance. These cigars have caps similar to handmades, long filler, and decent-quality wrappers. They can approach the experience of smoking a handmade cigar in flavor, though they wouldn't fool an experienced smoker.

Handmade cigars are so much more expensive than machine-mades quite simply because they take much longer to make, are labor-intensive, and use much more expensively produced and matured leaves. The handmaking process also leads to wastage.

THE CIGAR BOX

Cigars were originally sold in bundles covered with pigs' bladders (with a pod or two of vanilla to improve the smell); then came the use of large cedar chests, holding up to 10,000 cigars.

But in 1830, the banking firm of H. Upmann started shipping back cigars, for the use of its directors in London, in sealed cedar boxes stamped with the bank's emblem. When the bank decided to go, full-scale, into the cigar business, the cedar box took off as a form of packaging for all the major Havana brands, and all handmade cigars (though small quantities today are sometimes packaged in cardboard cartons, and single cigars of many brands come in aluminum tubes lined with cedar). Cedar helps to prevent cigars from drying out and furthers the maturing process.

The idea of using colorful lithographic labels, now used for all handmade brands, wherever they come from, started when Ramon Allones, a Galician immigrant to Cuba, initiated it for the brand he started in 1837. As the industry grew in the mid-19th century, so

H. UPMANN WAS AMONGST THE FIRST USERS OF THE CEDAR BOXES TO PACKAGE CIGARS.

did the need for clear brand identification. Labels or other illustrations also appear on the inside of the lids of many Havana and other brands. Boxes also usually have colorful decorative borders. The cedar box is sometimes referred to as a "boîte nature." Paper, usually colored, is normally glued to the interior of the box and is used to cover the cigars it contains.

Finally, after being filled and checked, the box is nailed shut and tightly sealed with a green and white label (a custom dating from 1912) to guarantee that the cigars are genuine Havanas. The practice of using a label, usually printed in similar colors and with similar wording, to seal the box continues today for most handmade brands, Cuban or not.

The Havana seal reads: "Cuban Government's warranty for cigars exported from Havana. Republica de Cuba. Sello de garantia nacional de procedencia."

Most sizes of the élite Cohiba brand come in varnished boxes, as do one or two of the larger sizes of a handful of other Cuban brands. The H. Upmann Sir Winston size, for instance, is available in a polished dark green box. These polished boxes are usually stamped with the brand symbol, rather than carrying any sort of label other than the government seal.

The form of packaging called 8–9–8 is used for some cigars in the Partagas and Ramon Allones brands. These boxes are polished, have curved edges, and contain 25 cigars, arranged in three layers with eight at the bottom, nine in the middle, and eight on top. Cigars with this sort of packaging are relatively expensive.

Cigar Box Stamps

The Havana seal.

The stamp telling you the cigars are handmade.

A prerevolutionary Havana box.

Hecho en Cuba has been stamped on the underside of Cuban boxes since 1961, when it replaced the English inscription "Made in Havana – Cuba." Since 1985, they have also carried a factory code and Cubatabaco's logo, the latter being replaced with Habanos SA from late 1994.

In 1989 the words "Totalmente a Mano" were added. Meaning "Totally by Hand," they provide the only cast-iron clue that the cigars are genuinely handmade in the traditional Cuban manner. "Hecho a Mano" or "Made by Hand" can cover a multitude of sins (European Union law permits cigars that are hand finished but machine bunched to be described as made by hand) – so the situation can be confusing.

Unless you have complete trust in your cigar merchant when buying older cigars, the only way to play safe is to buy post-1989 cigars with the "Totalmente a Mano" legend. If the box says: "Made in Havana, Cuba," it is almost certainly pre-revolutionary.

The factory code, on Havana cigars, is stamped in blue – using post-revolutionary factory designations. Thus, for instance:

JM stands for José Martí, formerly H. Upmann.
FPG stands for Francisco Perez German, formerly Partagas.
BM stands for Briones Montoto, formerly Romeo Y Julieta.
FR stands for Fernando Roig, formerly La Corona.
EL stands for El Laguito.
HM stands for Heroes del Moncada, formerly El Rey del Mundo.

Havana boxes also used to be stamped with the color of the cigars contained in them, but this practice has stopped, for the time being at least. Boxes, in the past, often read "claro," but this color classification was frequently inaccurate.

On non-Havana boxes, you might read "Envuelto a mano" – which only means hand-*packed*, but could deceive the unwary. "Hand rolled" means simply (as with Cuban "hand-finished" cigars) that the *wrapper* is put on by hand, the rest of the cigar is machine-made.

Underneath the boxes of American-produced cigars, there is normally a code: the letters TP, followed by a number identifying the manufacturer. Cigars imported into the United States don't show this code. Some cigars (Dominican Dunhills and the most expensive Macanudos, for instance) refer to a "vintage" on the box. This refers to the year of the tobacco crop, not the year of manufacture. Dunhills currently on sale, for example, are 1989 vintage – made from the Dominican 1989 harvest.

THE CIGAR BAND

The cigar band was introduced by the Dutchman, Gustave Bock, one of the first Europeans to get involved in the Havana cigar industry, somewhat after the introduction of the cigar box and labels, and for the same reason: to distinguish his brand from the many others on the market. His lead was soon followed by all the other brands, and cigar bands are still used by almost all handmade brands. When bands were originally introduced, other manufacturers followed Bock's example and had them made in Holland. Some cigars, sold in "Cabinet Selection" packaging – usually a deep cedar box containing a bundle of 50 loosely packed cigars tied together with silk ribbon – are sold without bands. This "half-wheel," as it is called, of 50 cigars is the way cigars were normally presented before the band was introduced. Some Honduran handmades are also often sold in Europe without bands (and usually singly), primarily for trademark reasons.

The band also has other minor functions, such as protecting the smoker's fingers from becoming stained (this was important when gentlemen wore white evening gloves) and, some claim, holding the wrapper together – though no decent wrapper should need help.

The cigar bands of older brands tend to be much fancier (with gold leaf in abundance) than those of modern brands. Those aimed at the very top of the market in particular – Cohiba, Dunhill, Montecristo, and Davidoff, for instance – are all simple and elegant.

The bands on non-Havana cigars with Cuban brand names tend to be similar to the Cuban originals, although they vary in small details (a typical one being that they bear the date of origin of the brand in the space where the Cuban version says "Habana").

Some Cuban brands use more than one band design, Hoyo de Monterrey, for instance, or Romeo Y Julieta, where the Churchill sizes have a simple, slim gold band, but other sizes have red ones.

The question of whether to smoke a cigar with the band on or off is purely a matter of personal choice. In Britain, it has traditionally been considered a matter of "bad form" to advertise the brand you are smoking, an inhibition which doesn't apply in Europe or the United States.

If you insist on removing the band, it is best to wait until you have smoked the cigar for a few minutes. The heat of the smoke will help to loosen the band from the wrapper and will make the gum on the band less adhesive and easier to remove. If you try to take the band off the cigar before starting to smoke it, you will risk damaging the wrapper.

CIGAR SIZES

There are countless cigar sizes. Cuba alone produces 69, 42 of which are for handmade Havanas. Each has a factory name, which usually bears no relationship to the name by which we know them, like Prominente (Double Corona), Julieta 2 (Churchill), Mareva (Petit Corona), Franciscano, Carolina, and so on. Some brands, Partagas for example, have 40 sizes, though several are machine-made. This is a throwback to the past when many selections were even larger. More modern brands such as Cohiba and Montecristo have just 11 sizes. Non-Havana brands tend to offer more manageable lines, although many, like Davidoff, which now boasts 19 sizes, have started to grow.

Sadly for the novice, there is no such thing as a standard size or a comprehensive list of sizes. Even the common Petit Corona can be found with different girths, and the name of Churchill covers a variety of alternative, albeit substantial, cigars. Listed below are the 25 most popular Havana sizes under their factory names. This may serve to indicate just how wide a selection is available, but it merely scratches the surface of the full panoply of choice offered by Cuba, let alone the Dominican Republic, Honduras, Mexico, and others.

The girth of a cigar is customarily expressed in terms of its ring gauge in $^{1}/_{64}$ths of an inch. Thus, if a cigar has a ring gauge of 49, it is $^{49}/_{64}$ths of an inch thick. Similarly, if a cigar had a ring gauge of 64, it would be an inch thick. Only a couple of cigars come into

CIGARS COME IN A BEWILDERING ARRAY OF SIZES AND SHAPES RANGING FROM THE 9¼-INCH GRAN CORONA TO THE 4-INCH ENTREACTO.

BASIC HAVANA SIZES

NAME	LENGTH: INCHES	RING GAUGE
	HEAVY RING GAUGE	
Gran Corona	9¼ inches	47
Prominente	7⅝ inches	49
Julieta 2	7 inches	47
Piramide*	6⅛ inches	52
Corona Gorda	5⅝ inches	46
Campana*	5½ inches	52
Hermoso No. 4	5 inches	48
Robusto	4⅞ inches	50
	STANDARD RING GAUGE	
Dalia	6¾ inches	43
Cervante	6½ inches	42
Corona Grande	6⅛ inches	42
Corona	5½ inches	42
Mareva	5 inches	42
Londres	5 inches	40
Minuto	4⅜ inches	42
Perla	4 inches	40
	SLENDER RING GAUGE	
Laguito No. 1	7½ inches	38
Ninfas	7 inches	33
Laguito No. 2	6 inches	38
Seoane	5 inches	36
Carolina	4¾ inches	26
Franciscano	4½ inches	40
Laguito No. 3	4½ inches	26
Cadete	4½ inches	36
Entreacto	3⅞ inches	30

* *These sizes, having pointed heads, are often referred to as "torpedoes." This name suggests, incorrectly, that they should be pointed at both ends. Cigars which are pointed at both ends are termed "Figuerados."*

this size today, the 9-inch long Royal Jamaica Goliath, and the same length José Benito Magnum from the Dominican Republic. The Casa Blanca Jeroboam and Half Jeroboam come with a whopping 66 ring gauge.

The largest properly smokable cigar made was Koh-i-Noor, made before World War II by Henry Clay for a maharaja. The same size, called the Visible Inmenso (18 inches long, 47 ring gauge) was made for King Farouk of Egypt. There was also once a panatela measuring 19½ inches. At the Partagas factory in Havana, they keep a collector's item: a cigar measuring almost 50 inches. You can also see a cigar a yard long with a ring gauge of 96 kept at the Davidoff store in London.

The smallest regularly made cigar was the Bolivar Delgado – measuring under 1½ inches.

There are plenty of variations to be found within a particular brand, particularly if the choice is large. Different brands, on the whole, tend to be expert at making different sizes. So, while the large ring gauge cigars in a certain brand might be excellent, you shouldn't assume that the smaller ones will either taste similar or be as well made. It comes down to actually trying the cigars.

SELECTING A CIGAR

As a general rule, cigars with larger ring gauges tend to be fuller flavored (there is normally more *ligero* and less *volado* in the blend), smoke more smoothly and slowly, and heat up less fast than those with small ring gauges. They also tend to be better made than the smaller ones (which are the sizes recently qualified apprentices start on). Cigars with small ring gauges often have little or no *ligero* tobacco in the filler blend. Large ring gauge cigars are almost always the preferred choice – if there is no hurry – of connoisseurs or experienced cigar smokers.

The beginner, however, is advised to choose a relatively small cigar, say a minuto or carolina, and then move up to the bigger sizes of a mild brand (see The Cigar Directory). Jamaican cigars, such as Macanudo (also made in the Dominican Republic), tend to be mild, or try H. Upmann among Havanas. A cervante is probably the best cigar above the corona size to move up to when you feel you have gone beyond the beginner stage.

A number of cigar experts, including the legendary Zino Davidoff, have pontificated about a person's physical appearance related to cigar size, and the Cubans have a saying, "As you approach 30, you have a 30 ring gauge; as you approach 50, you have a 50 ring gauge." This is, on the whole, so much hogwash. What size of cigar you smoke is entirely up to you and your pocket. Having said that, smoking a fat cigar, if you are very small or thin, can sometimes look rather comic or pretentious. But there is a case to be made about what sort of cigar to smoke at what time of day. Most smokers prefer milder, smaller cigars in the morning, or after a light lunch. The seasoned smoker, however, might go for something like a robusto after a heavy lunch – a lot of flavor packed into a reasonably short smoke. Certainly, most experienced smokers prefer a big, full-bodied cigar after a heavy meal or late at night, partly because a thin cigar will not last very long, and a mild one isn't so satisfying on a full stomach. So they will select a belicoso, Churchill, or double corona. By the same token, smoking a heavy cigar before dinner is likely to spoil your appetite and play havoc with your taste buds. Much the same consideration applies when people have strong drinks like port or brandy after dinner, rather than something lighter, which they will take before or during dinner. If you want to compare cigars, it is best to smoke them at similar times of day, taking meals and location into account, too.

When you choose a cigar, you should first make sure that the wrapper is intact (if not, reject it) and has a healthy sheen. You should also make sure that it isn't too dry or brittle (otherwise it will taste harsh) and that there is a noticeable bouquet (if not, the cigar has probably been badly stored). A good cigar should be neither too firm nor too soft. If the wrapper is heavily veined, the cigar should be rejected: quality control went wrong somewhere.

The color of a cigar's wrapper (and that part of the filler that you can see) will give you some clues, though it is not infallible since the filler blend is the key, as to its flavor. As a rule of thumb, the darker a cigar, the more full-bodied and (since darker wrappers contain more sugar) sweeter it is likely to be. Cigars, if properly stored, continue to mature and ferment in their cedar boxes. This aging process, during which a cigar loses acidity, is not unlike the maturing of good wine. Fuller-bodied cigars, particularly those with big ring gauges, tend to age better than milder ones. But it should be said that some full-bodied brands, such as Cohiba and Montecristo (apart, perhaps from the very largest sizes) don't age particularly well because the tobacco is fermented for longer – a complete extra fermentation in the case of Cohiba – in the factory, thus leaving little room for further maturation. There are even those who argue that if tobacco has been properly fermented, it is very unlikely to mature further (and if it has been fermented too little, it can't mature at all).

Milder cigars, particularly those with pale wrappers, will merely lose their bouquet if kept too long. In general, you should smoke lighter cigars before darker ones. Wrappers which are destined to age well start off oily, and get slightly darker and oilier as they mature.

Most importers of fine handmade cigars take care to age them a little before releasing them to the public (about two years for Havana cigars taken into Britain). There is no hard and fast rule about how long cigars should be left to mature (it can often be a matter of luck), but some experts state that cigars aged for six to ten years will be in the peak of condition. Others warn, quite rightly, that even if they are stored under ideal conditions, most cigars will lose their bouquet. If storage conditions are less good, they will also become dry. Even if well stored, it's probably sensible not to keep cigars for more than 10 years – by that time, they're unlikely to get any better, and will almost certainly have lost some of their bouquet.

Cigars should be smoked either within three months of manufacture or, failing that, not for at least a year after they are made. The intervening "period of sickness" as it is known – when the maturing process starts – is the worst time to smoke a cigar.

WRAPPER COLORS

Cigar wrappers can be classified into seven basic colors, although there are dozens of possible shades:

THE BASIC COLORS OF WRAPPERS RANGE FROM CLARO (PALE BROWN) TO OSCURO (BLACK).

Double claro (also called AMS, American Market Selection, or candela) – greenish brown (for instance, as in Macanudo "jade.") The color is achieved by picking the leaf before it reaches maturity and then drying it rapidly. Very mild, almost bland, with very little oil. Cigars with this color have traditionally been popular in the United States, but are very much less so today.

Claro – pale brown, like milky coffee. (For example, Havana brands like H. Upmann, or brands using Connecticut Shade wrappers.) The classic mild cigar color. The color is also called "natural," as is colorado claro.

Colorado claro – mid-brown, tawny. (For example, brands, such as Dominican Partagas, using Cameroon wrappers.)

Colorado – reddish dark brown, aromatic. This color is associated with well-matured cigars.

Colorado maduro – dark brown, medium strength, rather more aromatic than maduro. Usually gives a rich flavor, as found in many of the best Honduran cigars.

Maduro – very dark brown, like black coffee. (For example, full-bodied Havana brands such as Bolivar; cigars made with Mexican wrappers.) A color for seasoned smokers. Sometimes thought of as the traditional Cuban color.

Oscuro – more or less black. Very strong with little bouquet. Wrappers of this color, though once popular, are rarely produced today. These wrappers tend to be from Nicaragua, Brazil, Mexico, or the Connecticut Broadleaf (as opposed to Shade) type.

The darker the color, the sweeter and stronger the flavor is likely to be, and the greater the oil and sugar content of the wrapper. Darker wrappers will normally have spent longer on the tobacco plant or will come from higher altitudes: the extra exposure to sunlight produces both oil (as protection) and sugar (through photosynthesis). They will also have been fermented for longer.

The term EMS or English Market Selection is a broad one, which refers to brown cigars – anything other than double claro (AMS) essentially.

All handmade cigars need to be cut at the closed end before they can be smoked. Just how you do this is up to you. There are a number of cutters on the market ranging from small, cheap, easily portable guillotines (which come in single or double blade versions, the latter being the best), to fancy cigar scissors – which need some skill to use properly. You can use a sharp (that's essential) knife. If you use your fingernails, just pinch off the very top of the cap. The important thing is that the cut should be clean and level; otherwise, you will have difficulties with draw and risk damaging the wrapper. You should cut the cigar so that you leave about ⅛ inch of the cap. Piercing the cap isn't recommended: it interferes with the passage of smoke by compressing the filler, and will make the cigar overheat, leading to an unpleasant flavor. Cutters which make a wedge shape in the cap aren't recommended for the same reason. You should never cut a cigar on or below cap level: it is a certain way of ruining the wrapper. The idea is to take off just enough of the cap to expose the filler leaves. Whatever you use, make sure it is sharp.

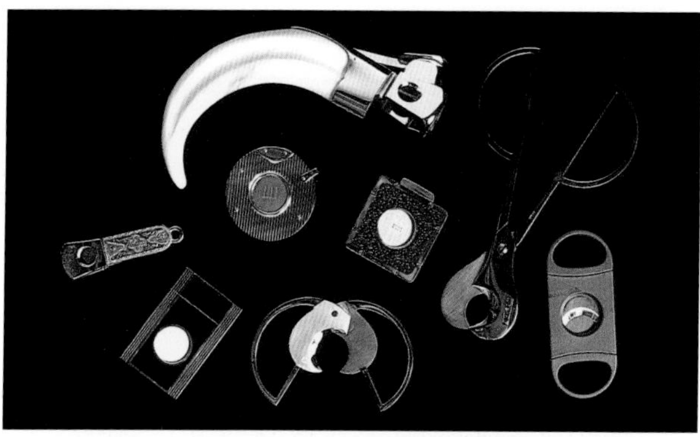

CUTTERS. THE GUILLOTINE TYPE IS THE SIMPLEST, CHEAPEST, AND BEST.

When you light a cigar you can use a butane lighter (though not a gasoline lighter, which will impair the flavor) or a match. There are special long slow-burning matches designed for cigar smokers available from high quality shops such as Dunhill or Davidoff, but a normal wooden match will do perfectly well. You should, however, avoid matches with a high sulfur or wax content. A properly lit cigar is always more enjoyable than one that isn't, so take it easy when you light one.

1 Hold the cigar horizontally, in direct contact with the flame, slowly revolving it until the end is charred evenly over its entire surface.
2 Only now do you put the cigar between your lips. Hold the flame about half an inch away from the end and draw slowly while turning it. The end of the cigar should now ignite. Make sure it is evenly lit; otherwise, one side will burn faster than the other.
3 Gently blow on the glowing end to make sure that it is burning evenly.

CUTTING A CIGAR. MAKE SURE IT'S NOT TOO NEAR THE BOTTOM OF THE CAP.

LIGHTING A CIGAR. DO IT CAREFULLY.

ALMOST READY TO SMOKE.

Older, well-matured cigars burn more easily than younger ones. If properly lit, the highest quality cigars have only a very narrow carbon rim at the lit end; mediocre cigars will have a thicker band.

To get the best out of them, cigars should be smoked slowly. They should not be dragged on or puffed too frequently. This will lead to overheating and spoil the flavor. Nor should the smoke – it hardly needs saying – be inhaled. The strong alkaline smoke and low nicotine content means that you will cough in reaction. A cigar like a corona will take about half an hour to smoke, with larger cigars taking an hour or more.

If your cigar goes out, don't worry: this is quite normal, particularly if you have already smoked half of it. Tap the cigar to remove any clinging ash. Then blow through the cigar to clear any stale smoke. Re-light as you would a new cigar. You should have a satisfactory smoke even if you leave the cigar for a couple of hours. Left much longer than that, it will taste stale, although a large ring gauge cigar smoked less than halfway down will still be smokeable, if not so enjoyable, the following day.

Cigars, unlike cigarettes, don't need to be tapped to remove the ash – it should fall off in due course. There is, on the other hand, no virtue in keeping a long cylinder of ash at the end of your cigar just because it is there: it impairs the passage of air and will make the cigar burn unevenly. The better the construction of the cigar, the longer and more "solid" will the ash cylinder be.

Once the cigar starts producing hot smoke and you get a strong aftertaste (usually when you are down to the last couple of inches), it is time to abandon it. As the French actor Sacha Guitry wrote: "If the birth of a genius resembles that of an idiot, the end of a Havana Corona resembles that of a five-cent cigar." It isn't necessary to stub out a cigar as you would a cigarette. Just leave it in the ashtray, and it will go out soon enough. Cigar stubs should be disposed of soon after they have gone out; otherwise, the room will acquire the lingering smell of stale smoke.

There are two things that really should not be done: first, don't roll a cigar near your ear. This is contemptuously known as "listening to the band" in the cigar trade. It tells you nothing at all about the cigar; second, you should never warm the length of the cigar before smoking it. This was originally done in order to burn off the rather unpleasant gum used to make some Seville cigars well over a hundred years ago. It is not necessary with today's high-quality handmade cigars, as they use a mere drop of flavorless, odorless vegetable gum.

2

THE CIGAR DIRECTORY

The selected list of handmade cigars in this section doesn't claim to be totally comprehensive, but it should contain most of the brands you are likely to come across. Some of them are only available in the United States, others only in Europe: but these things change. The same applies to sizes within brands (always listed in descending order of length).

Notes on flavor and aroma are necessarily subjective, but construction, draw, and wrapper quality can be more objectively assessed. You might love the flavor of a cigar even though it is criticized in the directory. It is, after all, a matter of personal taste.

C The country of origin of the cigar is denoted as follows:
Cuba, for example
Honduras, for example

F The categories for flavor range through four strengths:
Mild
Mild to medium
Medium to full-bodied
Very full-bodied

As for quality, the assessment takes into account appearance, construction, and consistency – the latter being of particular importance in any brand. Even so, cigars being handmade, and cigar tobacco being subject to the vagaries of climate (not to mention politics in some countries), things have changed and will change from time to time even for the best-known brands. These entries, then, can only be a guide, good for the time being.

Q The four categories for quality are as follows:
Could be better
Good-quality leaf and construction
Superior quality
The very best quality available

AFTER BEING ROLLED, CIGARS REST FOR 15 DAYS TO LOSE SOME OF THEIR MOISTURE.

ALIADOS

The band on every Aliados cigar bears the word Cuba. But it doesn't come from Cuba. It comes from Honduras. No doubt the hands that made it are those of a Cuban émigré. No doubt its production is supervised by ex-patriate Cubans, and no doubt the seeds for its tobacco are émigré Cuban seeds, but that doesn't make it Cuban.

In some ways, this is a pity because the cigars are good. They reflect the tireless devotion of that island's people to make fine cigars anywhere, and they possess the quality to stand on their own, no matter where they are from. The Piramide and Diademas shapes are masterpieces of the cigar-maker's art.

Most sizes come with a choice of Claro, Colorado Claro, and Colorado wrappers, which add interesting flavor alternatives to what is a medium to full-bodied taste. The Colorado has a particular richness.

SIZES

Name	Length: inches	Ring Gauge
Figurin	10 inches	60
Diademas	7½ inches	60
Piramedes	7½ inches	60
Churchill	7¼ inches	54
Cazadore	7 inches	45
Palma	7 inches	36
Corona Deluxe	6½ inches	45
Lonsdale	6½ inches	42
Toro	6 inches	54
No 4	5½ inches	45
Remedio	5½ inches	42
Rothschild	5 inches	51
Petit Cetro	5 inches	36

ROTHSCHILD : LENGTH 5 INCHES, RING GAUGE 51

CORONA DELUXE : LENGTH 6½ INCHES, RING GAUGE 45

LONSDALE : LENGTH 6½ INCHES, RING GAUGE 42

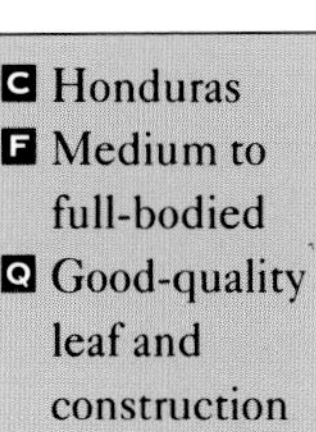

C Honduras
F Medium to full-bodied
Q Good-quality leaf and construction

ARTURO FUENTE

Cigar lore says that farmers raise tobacco and manufacturers make cigars. So, when the Fuente family, the largest producers of handmade cigars in the Dominican Republic, bought a plantation, eyebrows were raised on both sides of the divide. As word spread that the farm near El Caribe would grow wrappers, the same eyebrows arched. Virtually no one grew wrappers in the Dominican Republic and certainly not for premium cigars.

When a cigar wrapped with leaf from the El Caribe farm, now known as Chateau de la Fuente, topped *Cigar Aficionado's* autumn 1994 tasting, beating several Havanas before it even went on sale, the eyebrows hit the roof.

1995 saw the fourth crop harvested at Chateau de la Fuente, but by this book's press date, still no cigar created from its leaves has hit the market. These things take time in the opinion of Carlos and Carlito Fuente, but soon smokers and industry sceptics alike will be able to pass judgment on the Chateau de la Fuente Opus X series. (Sizes listed below.)

There are plenty of other Fuente cigars to enjoy in both their standard range and their Hemingway series of big figurados. Rare Colorado Cameroon wrappers are Fuente's hallmark, although some sizes like Royal Salute come dressed in "natural" Connecticut shade. All these cigars are well-constructed and well-blended, giving a distinguished light to medium flavor which reflects the enthusiasm of their makers. The Double Corona and Rothschild enclosed in cedar-wood wraps are particular favorites.

OPUS X SERIES

NAME	LENGTH: INCHES	RING GAUGE
Reserva A	9¼ inches	47
Double Corona	7⅝ inches	49
Reserva No. 1	6⅝ inches	44
Reserva No. 2	6¼ inches	52
Petit Lanceros	6¼ inches	38
Fuente Fuente	5⅝ inches	46
Robusto	5¼ inches	50

Petit Corona : Length 5 inches, Ring Gauge 38

Rothschild/Epicures : Length $4\frac{1}{2}$ inches, Ring Gauge 50

Privada No. 1: Length $6\frac{3}{4}$ inches, Ring Gauge 46

C Dominican Republic
F Light to medium
Q Superior quality

SIZES

Name	Length: inches	Ring Gauge
Canones	8½ inches	52
Royal Salute	7⅝ inches	52
Churchill	7½ inches	48
Panetela Fina	7 inches	38
Double Corona	6¾ inches	48
Privada No. 1	6¾ inches	46
Lonsdale	6½ inches	42
Flor Fina	6 inches	46
Cuban Corona	5¼ inches	44
Petit Corona	5 inches	38
Chateau Rothschild	4½ inches	50
HEMINGWAY SERIES		
Masterpiece	9 inches	52
Classic	7 inches	47
Signature	6 inches	47

ASHTON

Owned by a Philadelphia enterprise but named after an English pipe-maker of high repute, these well-tailored cigars are made in the Dominican Republic. They come in three styles of flavor. One is known simply as Ashton. Then there is Ashton Cabinet Selection and Ashton Aged Maduro. All three are wrapped in Connecticut leaf, although the Aged Maduro is in broadleaf rather than shade, and is filled with a Dominican blend.

The mildest are the Cabinet Selection, owing to extra aging of the tobaccos (the Nos. 1, 2, & 3 are tapered at both ends). For a mild to medium smoke, go for the standard selection in a size like the Magnum, or if sweetness appeals, try a Maduro No. 10.

The latest addition is a new style, the Ashton Crown series, using precious leaves from the Chateau de la Fuente farm.

SIZES

Name	Length: inches	Ring Gauge
Cabinet No. 1	9 inches	52
Churchill	7½ inches	52
Cabinet No. 10	7½ inches	52
No. 60 Maduro	7½ inches	52
Cabinet No. 8	7 inches	50
No. 50 Maduro	7 inches	48
Cabinet No. 2	7 inches	46
Prime Minister	6⅞ inches	48
No. 30 Maduro	6¾ inches	44
8-9-8	6½ inches	44
Elegante	6½ inches	35
Cabinet No. 7	6¼ inches	52
No. 40 Maduro	6 inches	50
Double "R"	6 inches	50
Cabinet No. 3	6 inches	46
Panetela	6 inches	36
Cabinet No. 6	5½ inches	50
Corona	5½ inches	44
No. 20 Maduro	5½ inches	44
No. 10 Maduro	5 inches	50
Magnum	5 inches	50
Cordial	5 inches	30

CABINET NO. 3 : LENGTH 6 INCHES, RING GAUGE 46

NO. 40 MADURO : LENGTH 6 INCHES, RING GAUGE 50

NO. 60 MADURO : LENGTH 7½ INCHES, RING GAUGE 52

Cabinet No. 2 : Length 7 inches, Ring Gauge 46

Prime Minister : Length $6\frac{7}{8}$ inches, Ring Gauge 48

Magnum : Length 5 inches, Ring Gauge 50

- **C** Dominican Republic
- **F** Mild to medium
- **Q** Good-quality leaf and construction

AVO

Avo Uvezian, accomplished musician and composer of *Strangers in the Night*, brings a clear understanding of harmony to the cigars which bear his name. Both in his standard selection and the more recent "XO" Series, the balance of flavor achieved between golden Connecticut wrappers and Dominican fillers and binders is well struck.

The "XO" Series, which can be identified by the two discreet letters on the side of the band, owes its premium price (no Avo is cheap) to a unique aging and fermenting process, although it is not clear quite what this entails.

The cigars are well constructed. The Pyramid and Belicosos sizes, however, should not be compared to the Cuban Piramides and Campana (often called Belicosos) sizes to which they bear little or no resemblance.

Flavors tend to intensify with the increase in girth of the cigars and can vary from a medium to a fuller, richer taste.

SIZES

Name	Length: inches	Ring Gauge
No. 3	7½ inches	52
Pyramid	7 inches	54
XO Maestoso	7 inches	48
No. 4	7 inches	38
No. 5	6¾ inches	46
No. 1	6¾ inches	42
No. 6	6½ inches	36
No. 2	6 inches	50
Belicosos	6 inches	48
No. 7	6 inches	44
XO Preludo	6 inches	40
XO Intermezzo	5½ inches	50
Petit Belicosos	5½ inches	46
No. 8	5½ inches	40
No. 9	4¾ inches	48

XO Intermezzo : Length 5½ inches, Ring Gauge 50

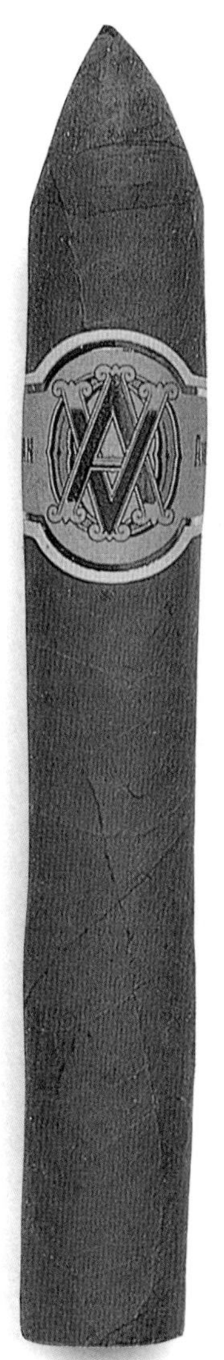

Petit Belicosos : Length 5½ inches, Ring Gauge 46

Pyramid : Length 7 inches, Ring Gauge 54

C Dominican Republic
F Medium to full
Q Superior quality

BACCARAT

Baccarats are full-bodied Honduran cigars, well made with medium brown Havana seed wrappers. They tend to be rather sweet – a wrapper quality which appeals to some and repels others.

SIZES

Name	Length: inches	Ring Gauge
Churchill	7 inches	48
No. 1	7 inches	43
Palma Fina	7 inches	36
No. 2	6¼ inches	43
Luchadores	6 inches	43
No. 4	5½ inches	42
Petit Corona	5¼ inches	39
Rothschild	5 inches	50
Platinum	4½ inches	32

C Honduras
F Medium to full-bodied
Q Good-quality leaf and construction

CHURCHILL : LENGTH 7 INCHES RING GAUGE 48

BANCES

A brand which comes in both hand- and machine-made sizes. The number of handmade sizes, all produced in Honduras from a blend of local tobaccos, has grown recently with additions like the weighty 8½ inch, 52 gauge President. The wrappers tend to be rather coarse, and tight rolling can give problems with the draw. Overall, these cigars offer a distinct, sweetish, slightly peppery taste at a keen price.

CORONA INMENSAS : LENGTH 6¾ INCHES, RING GAUGE 48

SIZES

NAME	LENGTH: INCHES	RING GAUGE
President	8½ inches	52
Corona Inmensas	6¾ inches	48
No. 1	6½ inches	43
Cazadores	6¼ inches	44
Breva	5¼ inches	43

C Honduras
F Mild to medium
Q Could be better

BAUZA

Echoes of pre-revolution Havana are still to be found on Bauza boxes, although today the cigars are made in the Dominican Republic. The wrappers are rich Colorado Cameroon. The Mexican binder combines with a mixture of Nicaraguan and Dominican fillers to deliver a very pleasant, aromatic smoke with a mild to medium flavor. The cigars are well put together by hand, but watch out for the Presidente (not listed below) which is short filler and not to be compared to the rest. Prices are very reasonable.

SIZES

Name	Length: inches	Ring Gauge
Fabulosos	7½ inches	50
Medalla D'Oro No. 1	6⅞ inches	44
Florete	6⅞ inches	35
Casa Grande	6¾ inches	48
Jaguar	6½ inches	42
Robusto	5½ inches	50
Grecos	5½ inches	42
Petit Corona	5 inches	38

C Dominican Republic
F Mild to medium
Q Superior quality

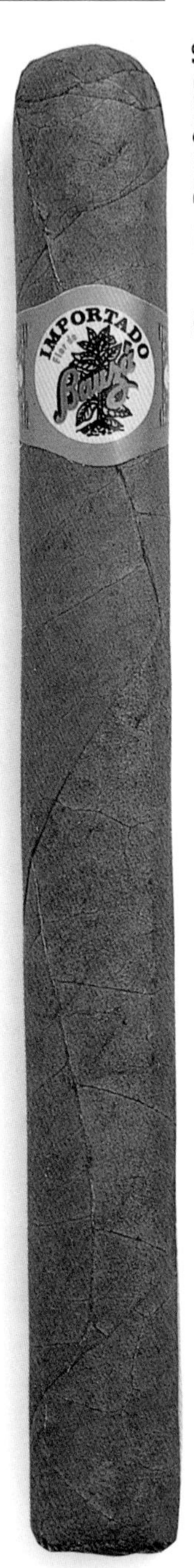

CASA GRANDE : LENGTH 6¾ INCHES, RING GAUGE 48

BOLIVAR

The famous Bolivar label and box featuring a portrait of the 19th-century Venezuelan revolutionary Simon Bolivar, liberator of much of South America from the Spanish empire, is one of the most instantly recognizable of all Havana cigar brands. At one time, the brand had the distinction of producing the smallest Havanas: the Delgado, measuring 1⅞ inches by 20 ring gauge, and even made a minute box of cigars for a doll's house in the royal nursery at Windsor Castle. It was founded in 1901 by the Rocha company.

There are some 20 cigars in the line, but many of the sizes come in machine-made versions, so be particularly careful if you think you've found a bargain. There are 19 handmade sizes, a selection of which is listed below. Bolivars are among the cheapest of handmade Cuban cigars and represent a good buy if – and this is a big if – their powerful flavor appeals to you, because as a brand, they are also among the strongest, fullest-bodied of Havanas. They are certainly not for the beginner, but appeal to many seasoned smokers. With their characteristic dark wrappers, they age well. Go for the larger sizes (Royal Corona upward) – which are well-constructed, draw and burn evenly, and have a strong aroma. The torpedo-shaped Belicosos Finos are a favorite with many, ideal after a heavy meal, whereas the mellow Royal Corona (robusto) is a very good post-lunch cigar. The Petit Corona is one of the fullest flavored available. The Palmas (panatela) which is produced in limited quantities should be avoided by those who expect a light smoke in this size. The distinctive Bolivar flavor comes not, as might be expected, because an unusually high proportion of ligero leaf is used, but because much more seco than volado is in the blend.

There are also Dominican versions of Bolivar on the market, not particularly noted, though good value, well made with Cameroon wrappers, and mild to medium in flavor. The Dominican line consists of only five sizes.

ROYAL CORONA : LENGTH 4⅞ INCHES, RING GAUGE 50

GOLD MEDAL : LENGTH 6⅜ INCHES, RING GAUGE 42

PETIT CORONA : LENGTH 5 INCHES, RING GAUGE 42

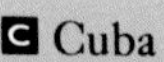

C Cuba
F Very full-bodied
Q Superior quality

C Dominican Republic
F Mild to medium
Q Good-quality leaf and construction

BELICOSOS FINOS : LENGTH 5½ INCHES, RING GAUGE 52

CUBAN SIZES

NAME	LENGTH: INCHES	RING GAUGE
Corona Gigantes	7 inches	47
Palmas	7 inches	33
Inmensas	6⅝ inches	43
Gold Medal	6⅜ inches	42
Corona Extra	5⅝ inches	44
Belicosos Finos	5½ inches	52
Corona	5½ inches	42
Petit Corona	5 inches	42
Bonitas	5 inches	40
Royal Corona	4⅞ inches	50
Corona Junior	4¼ inches	42

DOMINICAN SIZES

NAME	LENGTH: INCHES	RING GAUGE
Bolivares	7 inches	46
Corona Grand	6½ inches	42
Belicosos Finos	6½ inches	38
Panetelita	6 inches	31
Corona Extra	5½ inches	42

CANARIA D'ORO

Made in the Dominican Republic with Cameroon wrappers, these are well-made mild to medium-flavored cigars with a touch of sweetness. They come in medium-brown wrappers, except the very good Rothschild (robusto), which comes with a high-quality maduro wrapper. They are relatively good value for money and age well. The Vista size is tubed. The Corona size is well worth trying to get an impression of these cigars. They are neither particularly special, nor to be avoided.

SIZES

Name	Length: inches	Ring Gauge
Supremos	7 inches	45
Lonsdale	6½ inches	42
Vista	6¼ inches	32
Fino	6 inches	31
Immensos	5½ inches	49
Corona	5½ inches	42
Rothschild	4½ inches	50
Babies	4¼ inches	32

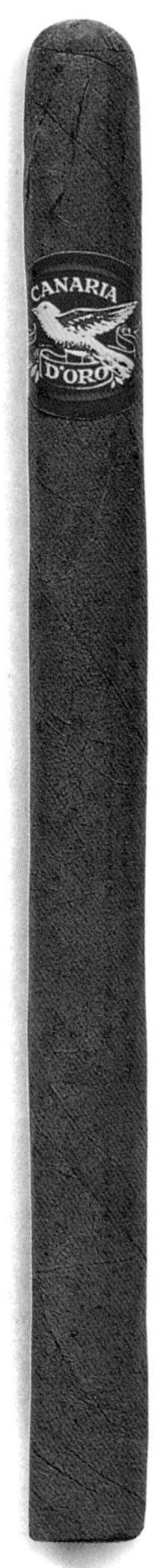

FINO : LENGTH 6 INCHES, RING GAUGE 31

LONSDALE : LENGTH $6\frac{1}{2}$ INCHES, RING GAUGE 42

ROTHSCHILD : LENGTH $4\frac{1}{2}$ INCHES, RING GAUGE 50

CORONA : LENGTH $5\frac{1}{2}$ INCHES, RING GAUGE 42

C Dominican Republic
F Mild to medium
Q Good-quality leaf and construction

Casa Blanca

Well-made Dominican cigars with Claro Connecticut wrappers on all sizes and maduro on some. The filler is Dominican and the binder Mexican. Casa Blanca's specialty is gargantuan cigars. The 10-inch Jeroboam and 5-inch Half Jeroboam have ring gauges over 1-inch thick (66). In general, the cigars are well-built (they must have some rollers with big hands), mild, and smooth. Just announced is a Piramide size, which may well measure up to the Egyptian original.

SIZES

Name	Length: inches	Ring Gauge
Jeroboam	10 inches	66
Presidente	7½ inches	50
Magnum	7 inches	60
Lonsdale	6½ inches	42
De Luxe	6 inches	50
Panetela	6 inches	35
Corona	5½ inches	42
Half Jeroboam	5 inches	66
Bonitas	4 inches	36

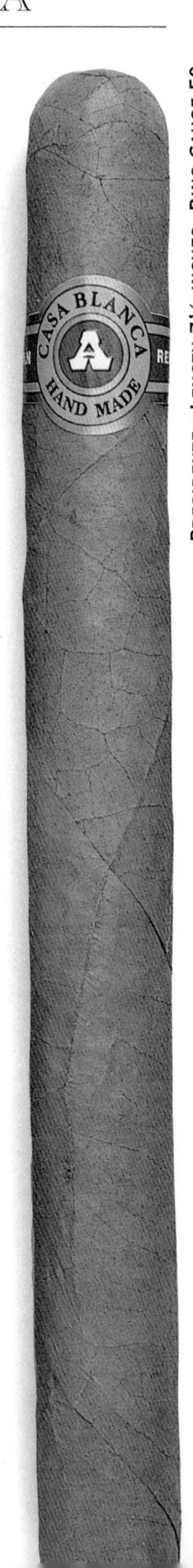

Presidente : Length 7½ inches, Ring Gauge 50

Magnum XL : Length 7 inches, Ring Gauge 60

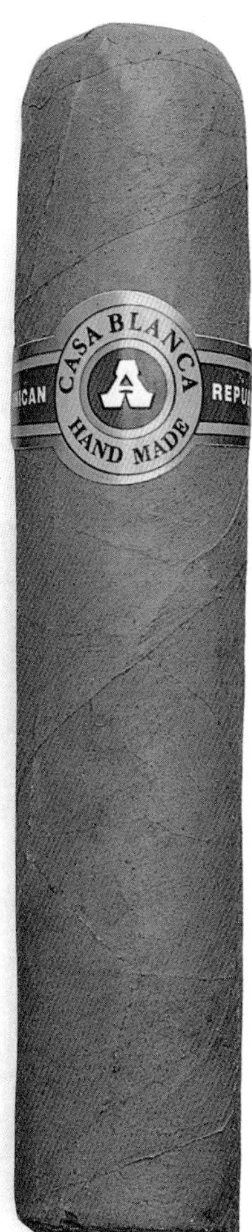

Half Jeroboam : Length 5 inches, Ring Gauge 66

Lonsdale : Length $6\frac{1}{2}$ inches, Ring Gauge 42

- **C** Dominican Republic
- **F** Mild
- **Q** Good-quality leaf and construction

V Centennial

The Roman five in V Centennial signifies that the brand was introduced to mark the passing of the five centuries since Columbus discovered tobacco. It also serves as a reminder that the cigars are made of tobaccos from five different countries. The wrapper is American (Connecticut), the binder Mexican, and the filler a mixture of Honduran for spice, Nicaraguan for aroma, and Dominican to round it off. The cigars are made in Honduras.

Creating and maintaining a successful blend of such diverse tobaccos is far from easy. Few attempt it. Creating a compatible and palatable balance is the problem, but when it is achieved, the resultant flavor can make a refreshing change. Overall V Centennial succeeds both in its claro form and particularly in its maduro, which is available in some sizes.

These cigars are handmade and well-constructed, although the wrappers can be grainy. The line, which tends toward larger sizes, is well-priced. Its Torpedo resembles a blunderbuss rather than the classic Piramide shape, but nonetheless it offers an interesting variation and smokes well.

SIZES

Name	Length: inches	Ring Gauge
Presidente	8 inches	50
Numero Uno	7½ inches	38
Torpedo	7 inches	54
Churchill	7 inches	48
Cetro	6¼ inches	44
Numero Dos	6 inches	50
Coronas	5½ inches	42
Robusto	5 inches	50

C Honduras
F Medium to full-bodied
Q Superior quality

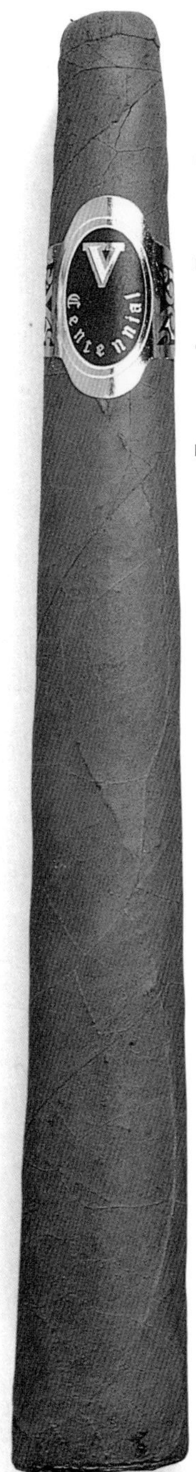

Torpedo : Length 7 inches, Ring Gauge 54

Cetro : Length 6¼ inches, Ring Gauge 44

Churchill : Length 7 inches, Ring Gauge 48

For a brand so young (founded in 1968) in the annals of Havanas, it is remarkable how many myths surround Cohiba. One affects its very name, which was said to be the aboriginal Taino Indian word for "tobacco," but is now understood to have meant "cigar." Another centers on Che Guevara's role in its creation. His portrait may hang above the Director's desk at the El Laguito factory, but since he quit his post as Minister of Industry in 1965 and perished in October of the year before the brand was born, his association with it could at best be described as fleeting. A third is that all Cohibas are made at El Laguito, which, although it was the case for over twenty years, is no longer so.

La verdad – the truth – about Cohiba's origin is now offered by Emilia Tamayo, the Director at El Laguito since June 1994. This charming and highly capable woman confirms that it all began in the mid-1960s when one of President Fidel Castro's bodyguards enjoyed a private supply of cigars from a local artisan. They so pleased the president that their creator, Eduardo Ribera, was asked to make cigars of his blend exclusively for Castro, under strict security in an Italianate mansion in the Havana suburb of El Laguito.

At first, the brand had no name, then in 1968, under the name Cohiba, production began of three sizes, each a personal favorite of the President – the Lancero, the Corona Especiale, and the Panetela. All were originals, so they were given the new factory names of Laguito No. 1, No. 2, which had the unique feature of a tiny pigtail on their caps, and No. 3.

For 14 years these three Cohibas were reserved solely for government and diplomatic use. However, the same sizes, using different blends, were adopted first by Davidoff as the No. 1, the No. 2, and the Ambassadrice when he was granted his brand in 1969 and then by Montecristo in the early 1970s as the Especial, the Especial No. 2, and the Joyita.

The guiding hand over this period, and indeed for 26 years, belonged to Avelino Lara. (He took over from Ribera in 1968.) Affable and relaxed, Lara, the eldest of four top-grade cigar rolling brothers, laid down the three principles which have made Cohiba Havanas the premier brand and, arguably, the world's finest cigar.

The first he calls "the selection of the selection." The produce of the top ten vegas in the Vuelta Abajo is put at his disposal. In any year he picks the five best for his wrappers, binders, ligeros, secos, and volados. The next is a special third fermentation, unique among Havana brands, which is applied to just two of the leaf-types – the ligero and seco. Moisture is added to the leaves as they age in barrels to ferment out the last vestiges of harshness. And third, the making of Cohibas is confined to the ablest rollers in Cuba, all of whom at El Laguito are female.

By 1982 word of this fabled cigar was out, and the decision was made to offer it to lesser mortals than the King of Spain and other such heads of state. Seven years later, three more sizes were introduced: the Esplendido (a Churchill), the Robusto, and the Exquisito, another unique size measuring 5 inches by 36 ring gauge. Of these, only the Exquisito is produced at El Laguito. The other two are made at either H. Upmann or Partagas.

More recently, to celebrate the 500th Anniversary of Columbus's discovery of cigars in Cuba, five new sizes known as the Linea 1492 (the six former sizes are now called the Linea Clasica) were first revealed at a celebration in Havana in November 1992, then launched at a glittering dinner at Claridge's Hotel in London a year later. Named Siglo (meaning century) I, II, III, IV, and V, the five centuries since Columbus are commemorated in a selection which bears more than a passing resemblance to some of the Davidoffs no longer made in Cuba. Crafted at Partagas, they are said to offer a lighter flavor than the Linea Clasica, which notably in its heavier sizes boasts a rare richness.

Cohibas made in the Dominican Republic can be found in a few American cigar stores. These bear no resemblance to the cigars above, but reflect an adroit move by General Cigar to register the name in the U.S. early in the 1980s. When the day of the repeal of the U.S./Cuban trade embargo finally dawns, contrary to the belief of many, Cohibas and virtually all other Havana brands will not flood onto the shelves of American cigar merchants. Instead, lawyers will rub their hands with glee as the battle to untangle one of the world's most complex trademark issues begins.

SIZES

NAME	LENGTH: INCHES	RING GAUGE
Lancero	7½ inches	38
Esplendido	7 inches	47
Coronas Especial	6 inches	38
Exquisito	5 inches	36
Robusto	4⅞ inches	50
Panetela	4½ inches	26

PANETELA : LENGTH 4½ INCHES, RING GAUGE 26

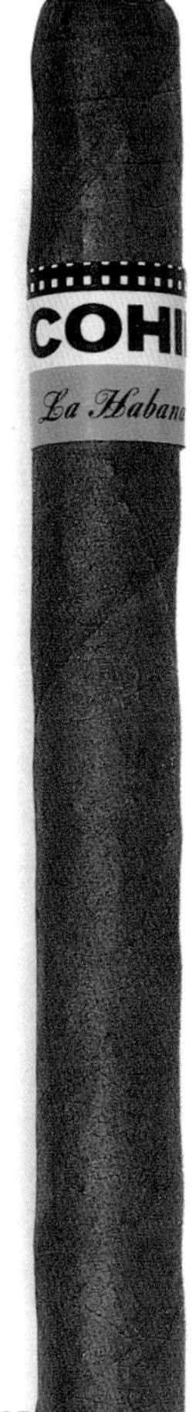

EXQUISITO : LENGTH 5 INCHES, RING GAUGE 36

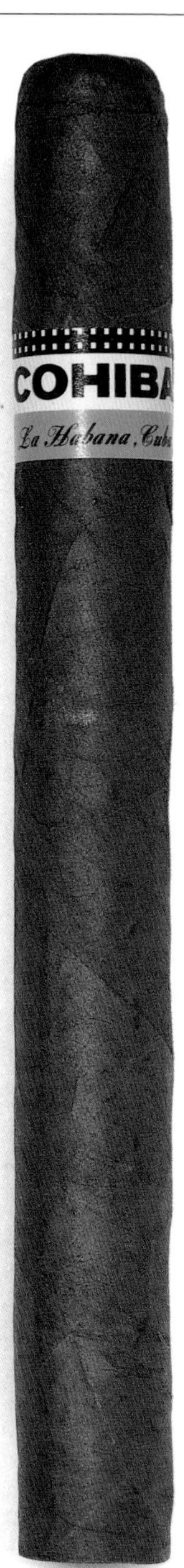

ESPLENDIDO : LENGTH 7 INCHES, RING GAUGE 47

EDUARDO RIBERA, CREATOR OF THE ORIGINAL COHIBA BLEND.

ROBUSTO : LENGTH $4\frac{7}{8}$ INCHES, RING GAUGE 50

CORONAS ESPECIAL : LENGTH 6 INCHES, RING GAUGE 38

LANCERO : LENGTH $7\frac{1}{2}$ INCHES, RING GAUGE 38

- **C** Cuba
- **F** Medium to full-bodied
- **Q** The very best quality available

SIGLO I : LENGTH 4 INCHES, RING GAUGE 40

SIGLO II : LENGTH 5 INCHES, RING GAUGE 42

EMILIA TAMAYO, EL LAGUITO'S DIRECTOR SINCE 1994, WITH RAFAEL GUERRA, HEAD OF CIGAR PRODUCTION.

SIGLO SERIES

Name	Length: inches	Ring Gauge
Siglo V	6⅝ inches	43
Siglo III	6⅛ inches	42
Siglo IV	5⅝ inches	46
Siglo II	5 inches	42
Siglo I	4 inches	40

SIGLO III : LENGTH 6⅛ INCHES, RING GAUGE 42

SIGLO IV : LENGTH 5⅝ INCHES, RING GAUGE 46

SIGLO V : LENGTH 6⅝ INCHES, RING GAUGE 43

Cuesta-Rey

The name of Cuesta-Rey dates back to the time when Tampa, Florida, was the American capital of a flourishing cigar manufacturing industry. Founded in 1884 by Angel La Madrid Cuesta, who was soon joined by Peregrino Rey, "clear Havanas" (cigars made in the United States from Cuban tobaccos) were their trade.

These days, Cuesta-Rey is presided over by the Newman family, owners of the last of the great Tampa cigar houses. They, too, have a proud history dating back a century and recorded in a recent book by tobacco historian Glen Westfall.

There are four series: Cabinet Selection: Centennial Collection, celebrating the founding of the brand in 1884; No. 95, commemorating the start of the Newman enterprise in 1895; and standard Cuesta-Rey, still made in Tampa, but by machine not hand.

Cabinet, Centennial, and No. 95 are all fully handmade in the Dominican Republic. Listed below is the Centennial Collection, a brand widely distributed throughout the world. These cigars are well put together using light Connecticut wrappers and Dominican binders. A veil of secrecy is drawn across the precise blend of filler by the family, but it seems that some Brazilian tobaccos are used. The flavor is mild, making it a perfect morning smoke.

Cabinet Selection also come with maduro Connecticut broadleaf wrappers and No. 95s use Colorado Cameroon wrappers.

SIZES

Name	Length: inches	Ring Gauge
Individual	8½ inches	52
Dominican #1	8½ inches	52
Dominican #2	7¼ inches	48
Aristocrat	7¼ inches	48
Dominican #3	7 inches	36
Dominican #4	6½ inches	42
Dominican #5	5½ inches	43
Captiva	6 3/16 inches	42
Cameo	4¼ inches	32

Dominican #1 : Length 8½ inches, Ring Gauge 52

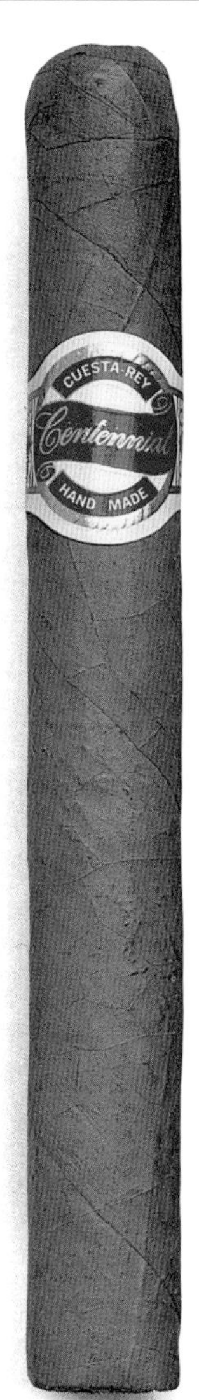

Dominican #5 : Length 5½ inches, Ring Gauge 43

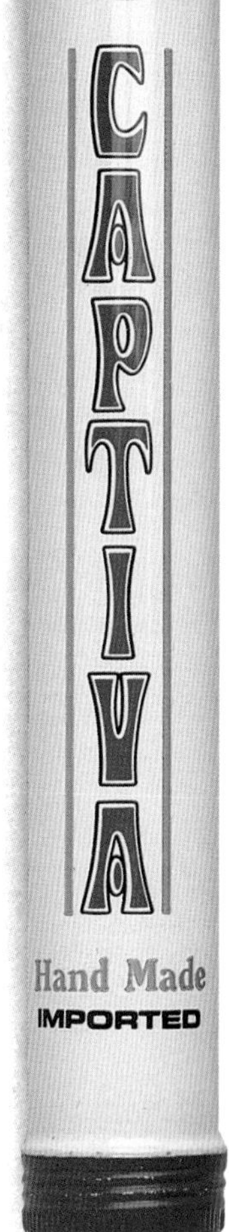

Captiva : Length 6$\frac{3}{16}$ inches, Ring Gauge 42

C Dominican Republic
F Mild
Q Superior quality

Davidoff is a byword for style and quality throughout the world. It encompasses men's fragrances, ties, glasses, cognac, humidors, and briefcases, but it is based upon cigars. To build such a multimillion dollar enterprise on a tobacco product in the late 20th century is a remarkable achievement, which owes its inspiration to Zino Davidoff and its present commercialisation to Ernst Schneider.

The life of Zino Davidoff, which ended in his 88th year on January 14, 1994, reads like a history of the 20th century. Born in Kiev, his family fled the pogroms to settle in Geneva and opened a tobacco shop where Lenin was a customer. Young Zino traveled the tobacco lands of Central and South America, ending up in Cuba, for which he formed a life-long affection. Amassing a hoard of Havanas from Vichy France, when World War II ended, he found himself with a rare stock of the finest cigars. His natural charm combined with a deep knowledge saw him first in 1947 create his Chateau selection based on Cuban Hoyo de Monterrey cabinets and then in 1969, aged 63, he was granted the accolade from the Cuban industry of a Havana brand.

His partnership with Ernst Schneider, one of several local Swiss importers at the time, dates from 1970. Schneider's Basel-based Oettinger Imex company saw the worldwide potential for the brand, and with Cubatabaco's expertise the cigar line was developed. There were three series of Davidoff Havanas, each with its own distinctive flavor. The fullest was the Chateau range, the lightest the Dom Perignon No. 1, No. 2, and Ambassadrice. In between there was the Thousand series.

THE EXTERIOR OF THE GENEVA BRANCH OF DAVIDOFF.

That these cigars should no longer be available is a tragedy born of a dispute between Oettinger and Cubatabaco, which resulted in the cessation of production of Davidoffs in Havana from March 1990 and the transfer of their manufacture to the Dominican Republic.

Much speculation has surrounded the reasons for the breakdown of what had been a highly successful marriage. It is perhaps best covered by Paul Garmirian in his book *The Gourmet Guide to Cigars.*

To their lasting credit, Davidoff and Schneider did not attempt to recreate the flavors of their former cigars. The sizes may be identical in many cases and the concept of different series with their own styles of taste is retained, but instead they have set out to create the very best of Dominican cigars. They accept that this will mean a lighter overall flavor, but believe that there are smokers who will be well pleased by it. Their success in several parts of the world suggests that they are right, but that is not to say that many previous devotees are not deeply disappointed.

DOMINICAN SIZES

NAME	LENGTH: INCHES	RING GAUGE
Aniversario No. 1	8 11/16 inches	48
Double R	7½ inches	50
Tubo No. 1	7½ inches	38
Aniversario No. 2	7 inches	48
3000	7 inches	33
Grand Cru No. 1	6⅛ inches	42
4000	6⅛ inches	42
Special T	6 inches	52
Tubo No. 2	6 inches	38
5000	5⅝ inches	46
Grand Cru No. 2	5⅝ inches	42
1000	5⅝ inches	34
Tubo No. 3	5⅛ inches	30
Special R	5 inches	50
Grand Cru No. 3	5 inches	42
2000	5 inches	42
Grand Cru No. 4	4⅝ inches	40
Ambassadrice	4⅝ inches	26
Grand Cru No. 5	4 inches	40

Dominican Davidoffs, dressed in their claro Connecticut wrappers, are immaculately tailored. The "Grand Cru" range replaces the former Chateau range by offering the richest flavor. The No. 1, No. 2, No. 3 (a new size), and Ambassadrice are as delicately mild as you can get, and the Thousand ("Mille") series are mild-flavored. There is an entirely new "Special" selection of heavier girth cigars, including the Special R (Robusto), the Special T (Piramides), and the latest, the Double R (Double Corona).

Finally, there are two sizes of Aniversario (the name first used for a limited edition Cuban cigar made to mark Zino's 80th birthday), which have a lightness remarkable in cigars of their size.

INSIDE THE DAVIDOFF SHOP, NEW YORK

C Dominican Republic
F Mild to medium
Q Superior quality

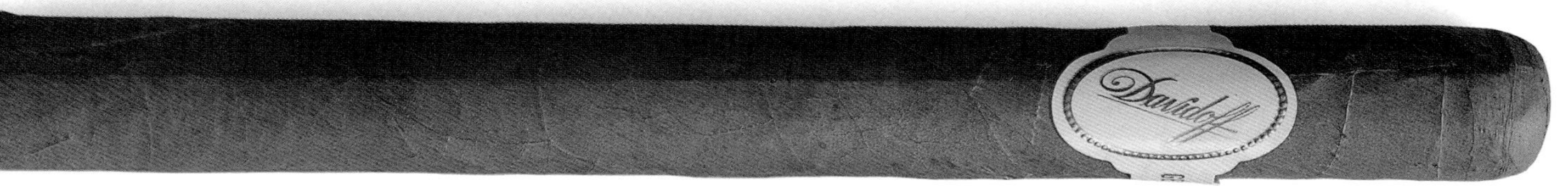

DOUBLE R : LENGTH 7½ INCHES, RING GAUGE 50

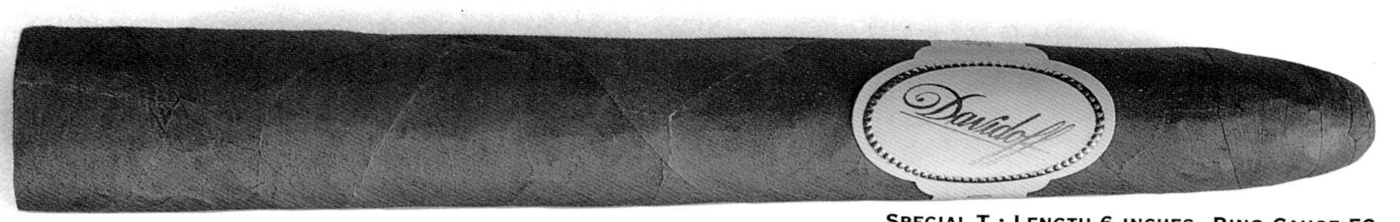

SPECIAL T : LENGTH 6 INCHES, RING GAUGE 52

TUBO NO. 2 : LENGTH 6 INCHES, RING GAUGE 38

DIPLOMATICOS

The Diplomaticos range was originally created for the French market in 1966. Although the brand's livery of a carriage and scrolls owes more to Walt Disney than to cigar tradition, it has been adopted recently by a Dominican Republic brand called Licenciados (also listed). The choice is limited, as is availability. They resemble Montecristos with a different label, and are cheaper.

Diplomaticos are very well-constructed, with a rich, but subtle flavor and excellent aroma. If you can find them, they are good value for the quality they represent. They are all good smokes, particularly No. 1, No. 2, and No. 3. The sizes, and numbering, are similar to the Montecristo range – though the line itself is smaller.

SIZES

Name	Length: inches	Ring Gauge
No. 6	7½ inches	38
No. 1	6½ inches	42
No. 2	6⅛ inches	52
No. 7	6 inches	38
No. 3	5½ inches	42
No. 4	5 inches	42
No. 5	4 inches	40

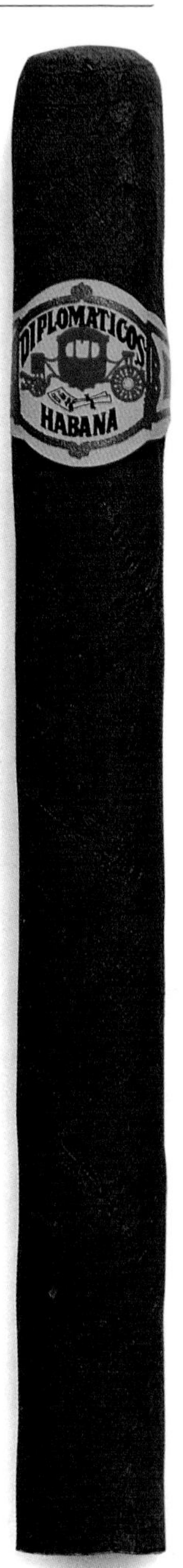

DIPLOMATICOS No. 1 : LENGTH 6½ INCHES, RING GAUGE 42

DIPLOMATICOS NO. 2 : LENGTH 6⅛ INCHES, RING GAUGE 52

DIPLOMATICOS NO. 3 : LENGTH 5½ INCHES, RING GAUGE 42

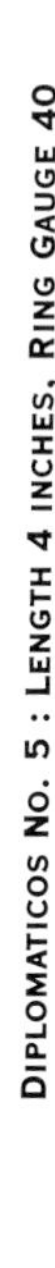

DIPLOMATICOS NO. 5 : LENGTH 4 INCHES, RING GAUGE 40

C Cuba
F Medium to full-bodied
Q Superior quality

Don Diego

These mellow mild to medium cigars (not too different from the rival Macanudo) are made in the Dominican Republic with claro and colorado claro wrappers. They are well made, and come in tubes as well as boxes. The brand was originally made in the Canary Islands – until the mid-1970s – and then had different characteristics. Connecticut wrappers are generally used, though some (mostly smaller) sizes come with fuller-flavored, sweeter-tasting, Cameroon wrappers. Some sizes are available in a choice of double claro (AMS) or colorado (EMS)

The Monarch tubes are very good of their type, as are the Lonsdales. The Royal Palmas and Corona Major are also tubed sizes. The Amatista size comes in a glass jar. Generally, with this brand, flavor, aroma, and burning qualitites are all high class. Don Diego Privadas are more fully matured.

SIZES

Name	Length: inches	Ring Gauge
Imperials	7 5/16 inches	46
Monarch	7 1/4 inches	46
Lonsdales	6 5/8 inches	42
Corona Bravas	6 1/2 inches	48
Grecos	6 1/2 inches	38
Amigos	6 1/2 inches	36
Royal Palms	6 1/8 inches	36
Grandes	6 inches	50
Amatista	5 7/8 inches	40
Corona	5 5/8 inches	42
Petit Corona	5 1/8 inches	42
Corona Major	5 1/16 inches	42
Babies	5 1/6 inches	33
Preludes	4 inches	28

Lonsdales : Length $6\frac{5}{8}$ inches, Ring Gauge 42

Corona Major : Length $5\frac{1}{16}$ inches, Ring Gauge 42

Grandes : Length 6 inches, Ring Gauge 50

- **C** Dominican Republic
- **F** Mild to medium
- **Q** Good-quality leaf and construction

Don Lino

First introduced in 1989, the Don Lino brand of handmade Honduran cigars has seen two new selections added in the last few years. The original blend covers fifteen very well-priced sizes wrapped in Connecticut shade and filled with a lightish mixture of Honduran tobaccos.

The seven sizes of the Habana Reserve line also come Connecticut wrapped and claim a special four year aging before reaching the market. This mellows their flavor but adds to the price.

Darker Connecticut broadleaf wrappers are used for the four heavy gauge sizes in the Colorado series launched in 1994. These also show signs of aging and have a pleasing mild to medium taste. Each size is available in its own humidor, which can be refilled from standard cedar boxes.

If well-filled cigars appeal, any Don Lino is the cigar for you. However, they are sometimes too well-filled, which can impede the draw.

COLORADO LONSDALE : LENGTH 6½ INCHES, RING GAUGE 44

- **C** Honduras
- **F** Mild to medium
- **Q** Good-quality leaf and construction

SIZES

NAME	LENGTH: INCHES	RING GAUGE
Supremos	8½ inches	52
Churchill	7½ inches	50
Torpedo	7 inches	48
Panetelas	7 inches	36
No. 1	6½ inches	44
No. 5	6¼ inches	44
No. 3	6 inches	36
Corona	5½ inches	50
Robustos	5½ inches	50
Toros	5½ inches	46
Peticetro	5½ inches	42
No. 4	5 inches	42
Rothschild	4½ inches	50
Epicures	4½ inches	32
HABANA RESERVE SERIES		
Churchills	7½ inches	50
Panetelas	7¹⁄₁₆ inches	36
Torpedo	7 inches	48
#1	6½ inches	44
Tubo	6½ inches	44
Toros	5½ inches	46
Robusto	5 inches	50
Rothschild	4½ inches	50
COLORADO SERIES		
Presidente	7½ inches	50
Torpedos	7 inches	48
Lonsdale	6½ inches	44
Robustos	5½ inches	50

DON MATEO

The wrappers of these Honduran cigars (all of them are available in mid-brown; a couple of sizes come in a choice of maduro) are somewhat veiny, rather coarse, and not of the best quality, but they are good enough, competitively priced cigars. They are well made (if rolled a little tightly), have a pleasant bouquet, and medium-bodied, peppery flavor with a hint of sweetness. They have a noticeable, if not particularly elegant, aroma.

SIZES

NAME	LENGTH: INCHES	RING GAUGE
No. 10	8 inches	52
No. 9	7½ inches	50
No. 1	7 inches	30
No. 6	6⅞ inches	48
No. 2	6⅞ inches	35
No. 8	6¼ inches	50
No. 3	6 inches	42
No. 5	5⅝ inches	44
No. 4	5½ inches	44
No. 7	4¾ inches	50

NO. 2 : LENGTH 6⅞ INCHES, RING GAUGE 35

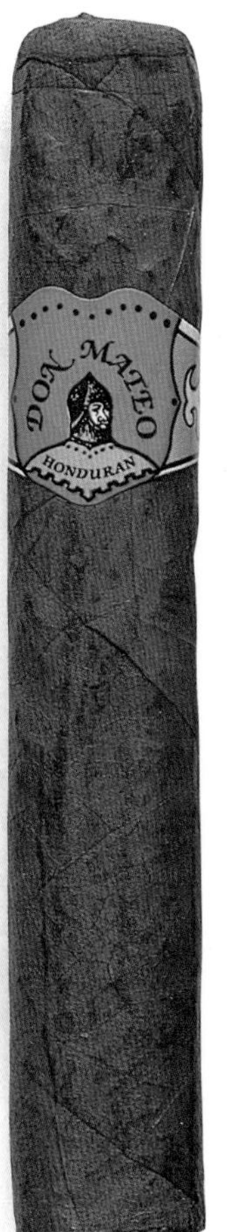

No. 7 : Length $4\frac{3}{4}$ inches, Ring Gauge 50

No. 8 : Length $6\frac{1}{4}$ inches, Ring Gauge 50

No. 9 : Length $7\frac{1}{2}$ inches, Ring Gauge 50

C Honduras
F Mild to medium
Q Good-quality leaf and construction

DON RAMOS

These well-made, full-flavored, 100 percent Honduran cigars are made in San Pedro de Sula, mainly for the British market. There are a total of seven sizes, all available in bundles. Five come in tubes and four in boxes. The bundles are simply numbered; No. 11 is a Churchill, No. 14 a Corona, No. 19 a Rothschild, and so on, and offer good value for money. The heavy gauge sizes – 6¾ inches, x 47 (Churchill/Gigantes/No. 11), 5⅝ inches x 46 (No. 13) and 4½ inches x 50 (Epicures/No. 19) are substantial smokes. All sizes have a spicy richness. The list below gives the bundle numbers.

EPICURE : LENGTH 4½ INCHES, RING GAUGE 50

SIZES

NAME	LENGTH: INCHES	RING GAUGE
No. 11	6¾ inches	47
No. 13	5⅝ inches	46
No. 14	5½ inches	42
No. 16	5 inches	42
No. 19	4½ inches	50
No. 20	4½ inches	52
No. 17	4 inches	42

C Honduras
F Medium to full-bodied
Q Superior quality

No. 16 : Length 5 inches, Ring Gauge 42

No. 14 : Length 5½ inches, Ring Gauge 42

No. 11 : Length 6¾ inches, Ring Gauge 47

Don Tomas

These are very well-made Honduran cigars which come in three lines at differing price levels. Special Edition incorporates five super-premium priced sizes using Honduran, Dominican, and Connecticut seed tobaccos grown near Talanga, Honduras. The International series offers just four sizes, identified by a distinctive slanting band, using an all Cuban-seed blend at a premium price. The standard series gives a choice of natural or maduro wrappers on a wide choice of sizes, including a so-called Corona with an unusually large ring gauge for this size, but a good smoke nonetheless.

Corona : Length 5½ inches, Ring Gauge 50

SIZES

Name	Length: inches	Ring Gauge
Gigante	8½ inches	52
Imperial	8 inches	44
President	7½ inches	50
Panatela Larga	7 inches	36
Cetro No. 2	6½ inches	44
Corona Grande	6½ inches	44
Supremo	6¼ inches	42
Panetela	6 inches	36
Toro	5⅝ inches	46
Corona	5½ inches	50
Blunt	5 inches	42
Rothschild	4½ inches	50

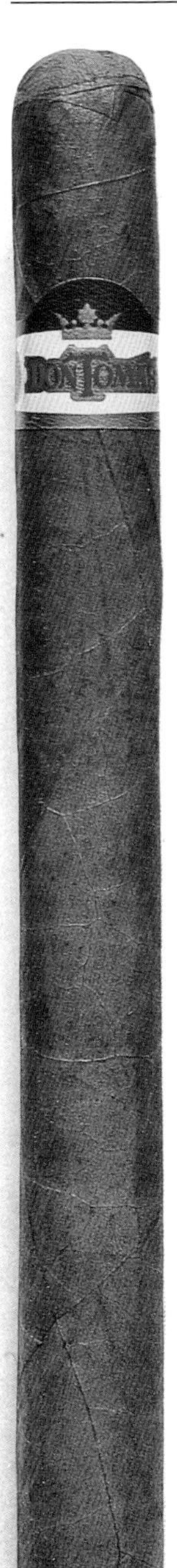

IMPERIAL : LENGTH 8 INCHES, RING GAUGE 44

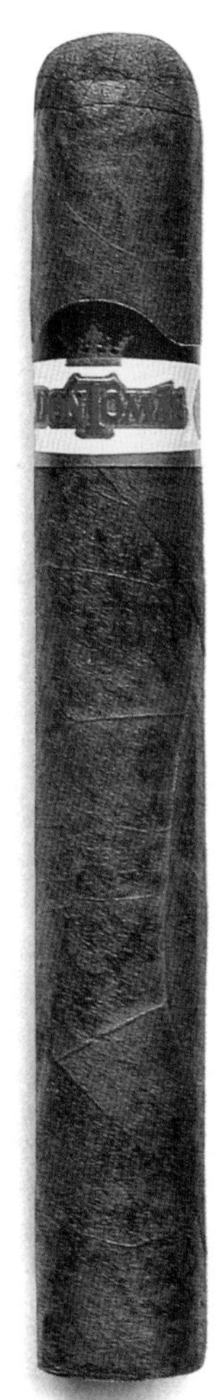

BLUNT : LENGTH 5 INCHES, RING GAUGE 42

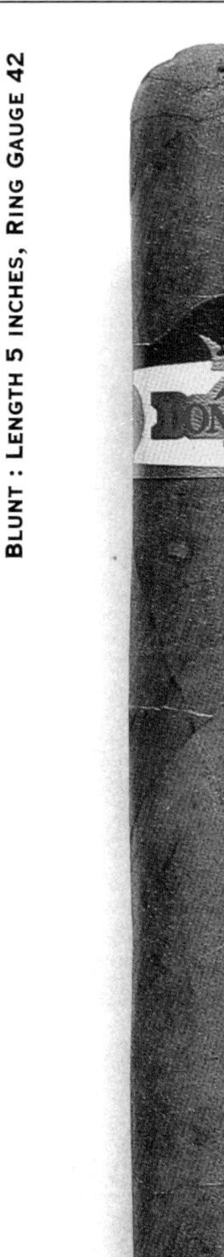

PRESIDENT : LENGTH 7½ INCHES, RING GAUGE 50

- **C** Honduras
- **F** Medium to full-bodied
- **Q** Superior quality

DUNHILL

The old English company of Alfred Dunhill can claim a long association with fine cigars. It was to Dunhill that the Menendez y Garcia company first took their infant Montecristo brand in 1935. There were house brands like Don Candido and Don Alfredo. The 1980s saw the brief creation of Dunhill's own brand of Havanas, sporting a red band bearing the company's elongated "d" logo on sizes like the Cabinetta, and Malecon.

Today Dunhill's accolade is reserved for two lines: one from the Dominican Republic – the Aged Cigar – which can be found throughout the United States, Europe, and the Middle East; and the other from the Canary Islands.

There are twelve sizes of Aged Cigars each made from Dominican fillers and wrapped in U.S. Connecticut leaf. Aged for a minimum of three months before they are distributed, these mid-priced cigars look good dressed with their blue bands and are well made and blended. They burn evenly and offer a distinctive, medium to full, but in no way heavy smoke, with a delicate aroma. Uniquely, a vintage is declared for this brand, based on the idea that its tobaccos are taken from a single year's harvest. The present vintage is 1989, although some of the 1987 vintage may still be found.

The Canary Islands selection is smaller, numbering just five sizes. Distinguished by their black bands, these cigars offer a mild to medium flavor with a touch of sweetness. They, too, are well constructed, but offer a somewhat rougher, less polished smoke.

DOMINICAN SIZES

Name	Length: inches	Ring Gauge
Peravias	7 inches	50
Cabreras	7 inches	48
Fantinos	7 inches	28
Diamantes	6⅝ inches	42
Samanas	6½ inches	38
Condados	6 inches	48
Tabaras	5 9/16 inches	42
Valverdes	5½ inches	42
Altamiras	5 inches	48
Romanas	4½ inches	50
Bavaros	4½ inches	28
Caletas	4 inches	42

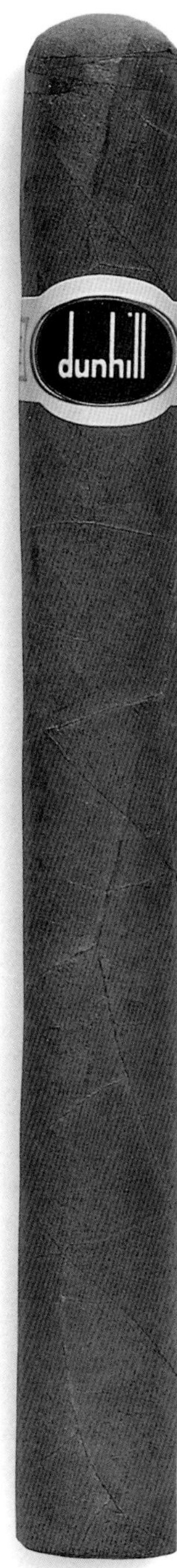

PERAVAIS : LENGTH 7 INCHES, RING GAUGE 50

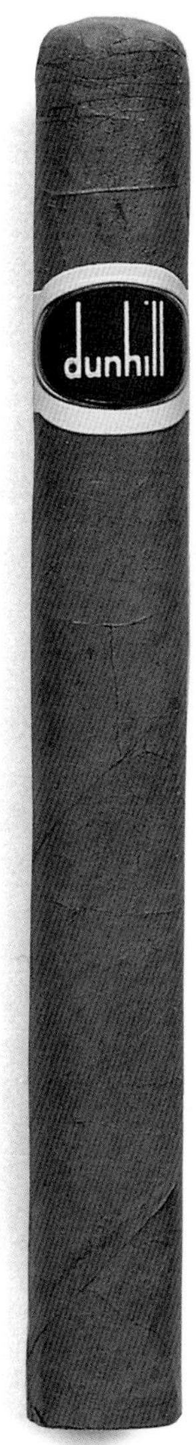

VALVERDES : LENGTH $5\frac{1}{2}$ INCHES, RING GAUGE 42

DIAMANTES : LENGTH $6\frac{5}{8}$ INCHES, RING GAUGE 42

C Dominican Republic
F Medium to full-bodied
Q Superior quality

CANARY ISLANDS SIZES

NAME	LENGTH: INCHES	RING GAUGE
Lonsdale Grande	7½ inches	42
Corona Grandes	6½ inches	42
Panetela	6⅛ inches	30
Corona Extra	5¹¹⁄₁₆ inches	50
Corona	5½ inches	42

C Canary Islands
F Mild to medium
Q Good-quality leaf and construction

PANETELA : LENGTH 6⅛ INCHES, RING GAUGE 30

CORONA EXTRA : LENGTH 5¹¹⁄₁₆ INCHES, RING GAUGE 50

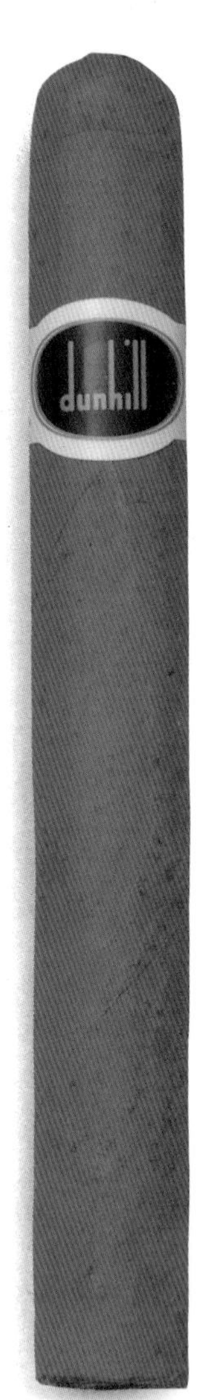

CORONA : LENGTH 5½ INCHES, RING GAUGE 42

El Rey Del Mundo

The name means "King of the World," a confident enough title for this brand, originally founded in 1882 by the Antonio Allones company. Many connoisseurs would rate it among their favorite brands. The selection is large, with some sizes available in machine-made versions. They are made in the Romeo Y Julieta factory along with other medium-flavored brands. There are also well-made (but much fuller-bodied) Honduran versions in 26 sizes (a selection is listed below) from JR Tobacco with completely different names such as Flor de Llaneza, Imperiale, and Montecarlo, although they also list a Choix Supereme. Some contain a Dominican filler for a lighter flavor, aimed at the less-experienced smoker.

The El Rey del Mundo Corona was the favorite cigar of film producer Darryl F. Zanuck – former head of 20th Century-Fox – who once actually owned a plantation in Cuba. The British tycoon Sir Terence Conran is also a fan.

The Cuban are a well-constructed, high-quality line of cigars, with smooth, oily wrappers, particularly the larger sizes (Tainos, Choix Supreme, Gran Corona, and above). Even the larger sizes are light and medium to mild (too mild for those for whom big cigars mean body), and the aroma is always subtle. These are good beginners' cigars, and very suitable for daytime smoking; even the larger sizes wouldn't be best appreciated after a heavy dinner.

CUBAN SIZES

Name	Length: inches	Ring Gauge
Tainos	7 inches	47
Lonsdale	6½ inches	42
Gran Corona	5½ inches	46
Isabel	5½ inches	43
Corona De Luxe	5½ inches	42
Choix Supreme	5 inches	49
Petit Corona	5 inches	42
Demi Tasse	4 inches	30

CUBAN SIZES

Name	Length: inches	Ring Gauge
Coronation	8½ inches	52
Principle	8 inches	47
Flor del Mundo	7¼ inches	54
Robusto Suprema	7¼ inches	54
Imperiale	7¼ inches	54
Corona Immensa	7¼ inches	47
Double Corona	7 inches	49
Cedar	7 inches	43
Flor de Llaneza	6½ inches	54
Plantation	6½ inches	30
Montecarlo	6⅛ inches	48
Robusto Larga	6 inches	54
Originale	5⅝ inches	45
Classic Corona	5⅝ inches	45
Corona	5⅝ inches	45
Rectangulare	5⅝ inches	45
Habana Club	5½ inches	42
*Tino	5½ inches	38
*Elegante	5⅜ inches	29
Choix Supreme	5 inches	49
*Reynita	5 inches	38
Robusto	5 inches	54
Robusto Zavalla	5 inches	54
Rothschilde	5 inches	50
*Petit Lonsdale	4⅝ inches	43
Cafe au Lait	4½ inches	35

*Lighter Dominican filler

C Cuba
F Mild to medium
Q Superior quality

Choix Supreme : Length 5 inches, Ring Gauge 49

Cafe au Lait : Length 4½ inches, Ring Gauge 35

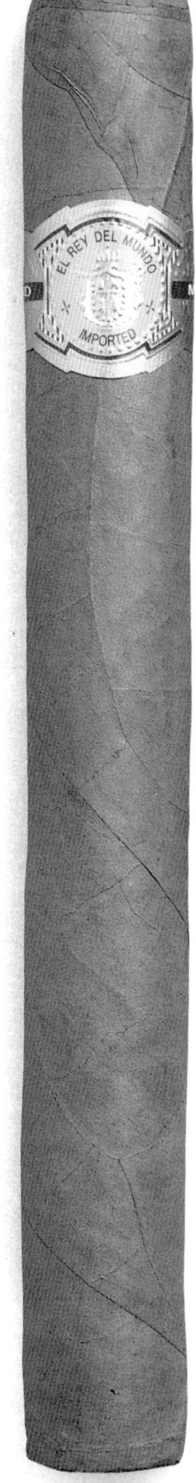

Flor Del Mundo : Length 7¼ inches, Ring Gauge 54

C Honduras
F Medium to full-bodied
Q Good-quality leaf and construction

EXCALIBUR

Excaliburs are the very best of the Hoyo de Monterrey brand made by Villazon from Havana seed wrappers in Honduras (see also Hoyo de Monterrey entry). They are medium to full-bodied, rich, extremely well made, and among the best non-Cuban cigars on the market. They are sold with the Hoyo de Monterrey label in the United States (with the additional word Excalibur at the bottom of the band), but simply as Excalibur in Europe, for trademark reasons. Try the No. II.

SIZES

NAME	LENGTH: INCHES	RING GAUGE
No. I	7¼ inches	54
Banquet	6¾ inches	48
No. II	6¾ inches	47
No. III	6⅛ inches	50
No. V	6⅛ inches	44
No. IV	5⅝ inches	45
No. VI	5⅜ inches	38
No. VII	5 inches	43

C Honduras
F Medium to full-bodied
Q Superior quality

NO. I : LENGTH 7¼ INCHES, RING GAUGE 54

No. III : Length 6⅛ inches, Ring Gauge 50

No. IV : Length 5⅝ inches, Ring Gauge 45

No. V : Length 6⅛ inches, Ring Gauge 44

FONSECA

Boxes of Cuban Fonsecas feature both New York's Statue of Liberty and Havana's Morro Castle, indicating that the brand was born at a time when relations between these two great cities were easier than they are today.

Since 1965, the brand has also been made in the Dominican Republic, originally using Cameroon wrappers, but now preferring light Connecticut shade. Mexican binders combine with Dominican fillers in very well-made cigars for a truly mild smoke.

The small range of Cuban Fonsecas come uniquely encased in white tissue. They are Barcelona's favorite cigar, where prodigious quantities are consumed by people who know their smokes. The flavor is light to medium with a slight saltiness.

DOMINICAN SIZES

Name	Length: inches	Ring Gauge
#10–10	7 inches	50
#7–9–9	6½ inches	46
#8–9–9	6 inches	43
Triangular	5½ inches	56
#5–50	5 inches	50
#2–2	4¼ inches	40

CUBAN SIZES

Name	Length: inches	Ring Gauge
No. 1	6⅜ inches	44
Cosacos	5¼ inches	40
Invictos	5¼ inches	45
Delicias	4⅞ inches	40
K.D.T. Cadetes	4½ inches	36

#10–10 : Length 7 inches, Ring Gauge 50

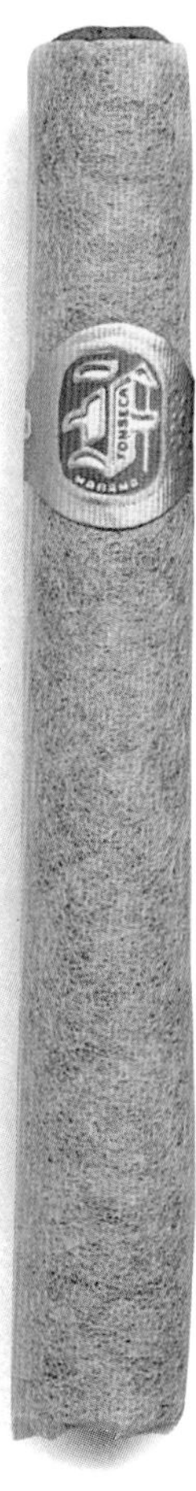

K.D.T. CADETES : LENGTH 4½ INCHES, RING GAUGE 36

COSACOS : LENGTH 5¼ INCHES, RING GAUGE 40

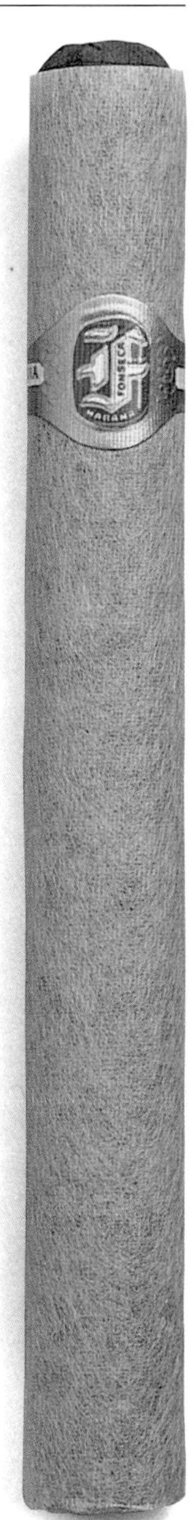

NO 1 : LENGTH 6⅜ INCHES, RING GAUGE 44

C Cuba
F Mild to medium
Q Good-quality leaf and construction

C Dominican Republic
F Mild
Q Superior quality

GISPERT

This is an old Havana brand – originally produced in Pinar del Rio – but there are now only three handmade sizes available (and one machine-made). They aren't easy to come by (the brand is disappearing fast, and only easily available in Havana), but provide a light, possibly dull, smoke suitable for the beginner. Good daytime smokes, but nothing more, for the initiated. Well-made, but more a collector's item than a must for smoking.

SIZES

NAME	LENGTH: INCHES	RING GAUGE
Corona	5⅝ inches	42
Petit Corona de Luxe	5 inches	42
Habaneras No. 2	4⅝ inches	35

C Cuba
F Mild
Q Good-quality leaf and construction

CORONA : LENGTH 5⅝ INCHES, RING GAUGE 42

GRIFFIN'S

Griffin is the brainchild of Geneva-based Bernard H. Grobet, an early disciple of Zino Davidoff. He was among the first Europeans who over a decade ago saw the potential for cigars made in the Dominican Republic. More recently, both the manufacture and marketing of the brand have come under the influence of his old mentor's organization – Davidoff & Cie. The cigars look good in their light Connecticut wrappers and are well-constructed. The flavor is as to be expected from Dominican filler in this presentation, and they are quite costly.

SIZES

NAME	LENGTH: INCHES	RING GAUGE
Don Bernardo	9 inches	46
Prestige	8 inches	48
No. 200	7 inches	44
No. 100	7 inches	38
No. 300	6¼ inches	44
No. 400	6 inches	38
Privilege	5 inches	30
Griffinos	3¾ inches	18

C Dominican Republic
F Mild to medium
Q Superior quality

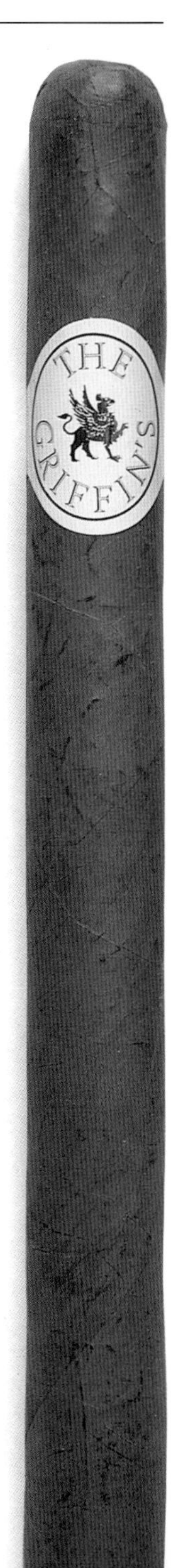

PRESTIGE : LENGTH 8 INCHES, RING GAUGE 48

H. UPMANN

Herman Upmann was a member of a European banking family and a lover of good cigars. It came as no surprise when, in around 1840, he volunteered to open a branch of the bank in Havana. The cigars he sent home proved so popular that, in 1844, he invested in a cigar factory. The company traded successfully as both bankers and cigar makers until 1922, when first the bank and then the cigar business failed. A British firm, J. Frankau & Co. saved the cigar brand and ran the factory until 1935 when it was sold to the newly founded Menendez y Garcia company.

In 1944 a new H. Upmann factory was opened in Old Havana's Calle Amistad to mark the centenary of Herman's enterprise. The brand is made there to this day, at present, under the direction of the talented Benito Molina.

Havana Upmanns are mild to medium-flavored, very smooth, subtle cigars. They are generally very satisfactory, although sometimes, particularly when they are machine-made, let down by construction and burning qualities, occasionally overheating and leaving a bitter aftertaste. They are, however, a good beginner's cigar, or one to be smoked after a light meal. Cuban Upmanns come in a bewildering choice of over 30 sizes, many of them similar to one another. A number of Upmann sizes (including machine-mades – so beware) are sold in tubes. Only handmade Upmanns are imported into Britain, however.

Handmade cigars bearing the Upmann name are also produced by the Consolidated Cigar Corporation in the Dominican Republic, with Cameroon wrappers and Latin American fillers. They are a very respectable, well-made, mild to medium smoke, usually in oily colorado wrappers. The 12 boxed sizes available include Corona Imperiales, Lonsdale, Corona, Petit Corona, and Churchill. There are also six tubed sizes. The label on non-Havana Upmanns reads: "H. Upmann 1844," whereas the Cuban version says: "H. Upmann Habana." The sizes given below are the standard Havana versions.

CUBAN SIZES

NAME	LENGTH: INCHES	RING GAUGE
Monarchs	7 inches	47
Monarcas (also called Sir Winston)	7 inches	47
Lonsdale (and No. 1)	6½ inches	42
Upmann No. 2	6⅛ inches	52
Grand Corona	5¾ inches	40
Magnum	5½ inches	46
Corona	5½ inches	42
Royal Corona	5½ inches	42
Corona Major	5⅛ inches	42
Connoisseur No. 1	5 inches	48
Petit Corona (and No. 4)	5 inches	42
Corona Junior	4½ inches	36
Petit Upmann	4½ inches	36

UPMANN NO. 2 : LENGTH $6\frac{1}{8}$ INCHES, RING GAUGE 52

PETIT UPMANN : LENGTH $4\frac{1}{2}$ INCHES, RING GAUGE 36

LONSDALE (AND NO. 1) ; LENGTH $6\frac{1}{2}$ INCHES, RING GAUGE 42

C Cuba
F Mild
Q Superior quality

PEQUENOS NO. 100 : LENGTH 4½ INCHES, RING GAUGE 50

AMATISTA : LENGTH 5⅞ INCHES, RING GAUGE 42

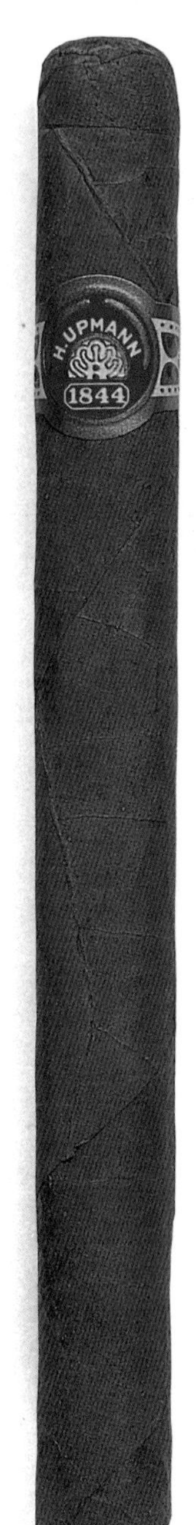

LONSDALE : LENGTH 6⅝ INCHES, RING GAUGE 42

C Dominican Republic
F Mild to medium
Q Good-quality leaf and construction

HENRY CLAY

This was one of the most famous of the old Havana brands, dating back to the 19th century and named after an American senator with business interests in Cuba. In the 1930s, its manufacture was transferred from Havana to Trenton, New Jersey, to avoid the exuberance of the Cuban workforce. The brand is now made in the Dominican Republic. There are only three sizes, all medium to full-bodied with mid-brown wrappers.

SIZES

NAME	LENGTH: INCHES	RING GAUGE
Breva Fina	6½ inches	48
Breva Conserva	5⅝ inches	46
Breva	5½ inches	42

C Dominican Republic
F Medium to full-bodied
Q Good-quality leaf and construction

BREVA : LENGTH 5½ INCHES, RING GAUGE 42

BREVA CONSERVA : LENGTH 5⅝ INCHES, RING GAUGE 46

BREVA FINA : LENGTH 6½ INCHES, RING GAUGE 48

HOYO DE MONTERREY

There is an old wrought-iron gate overlooking a square in the Vuelta Abajo village of San Juan y Martinez which bears the inscription "Hoyo de Monterrey: Jose Gener 1860." It leads to one of Cuba's most renowned "vegas finas," a plantation specializing in sun-grown tobaccos for binders and fillers. Here, Jose Gener started his career as a leaf grower on prime land (a "hoyo" is a dip in a field much favored by farmers for reasons of drainage) before founding the Hoyo de Monterrey brand in 1865.

Hoyo's flagship, the Double Corona, has become a unit of exchange among cigar lovers with a value far exceeding precious metals and usually only transacted as a token of close friendship. It has a delicacy of flavor combined with a richness of taste which is a credit to the blenders and rollers at the La Corona factory where it is made. It is felt that other Hoyo sizes, some of which are machine-made, do not live up to their champion. There is some truth in this, but the Epicure Nos. 1 & 2, particularly in 50 bundles, are clear exceptions. It should also be remembered that Zino Davidoff first created his Chateau range using cabinet selection Hoyos in standard sizes. Davidoff's early success in Switzerland inspired the creation in 1970, by a rival merchant, of the Le Hoyo series, which has a spicier, somewhat fuller flavor.

This pales into significance however alongside the brand of cigars bearing the same name made in Honduras. What these cigars lack in fine tailoring, they make up for in sheer flavor. They are an

CUBAN SIZES

NAME	LENGTH: INCHES	RING GAUGE
Particulares	9¼ inches	47
Double Corona	7½ inches	49
Churchill	7 inches	47
Le Hoyo des Dieux	6⅛ inches	42
Le Hoyo du Dauphin	6 inches	38
Epicure No. 1	5⅝ inches	46
Jeanne D'Arc	5⅝ inches	35
Le Hoyo du Roi	5½ inches	42
Corona	5½ inches	42
Le Hoyo du Prince	5 inches	40
Epicure No. 2	4⅞ inches	50
Margarita	4¾ inches	26

"espresso" of a cigar, particularly in the larger girth sizes like the Rothschild and Governors. They are made by men who clearly appreciate the taste of tobacco.

It is important not to confuse the standard Honduran Hoyo line with the Excalibur series (also listed). These are sold as Hoyo de Monterrey Excalibur in the United States, but for trademark reasons, the Hoyo connection is dropped in Europe. They are among the finest of cigars and have a different style of flavor.

HONDURAN SIZES

NAME	LENGTH: INCHES	RING GAUGE
Presidents	8½ inches	52
Sultans	7¼ inches	54
Cuban Largos	7¼ inches	47
Largo Elegantes	7¼ inches	34
Cetros	7 inches	43
Double Corona	6¾ inches	48
No. 1	6½ inches	43
Churchills	6¼ inches	45
Ambassadors	6¼ inches	44
Delights	6¼ inches	37
Governors	6⅛ inches	50
Culebras	6 inches	35
Coronas	5⅝ inches	46
Cafe Royales	5⅝ inches	43
Dreams	5¾ inches	46
Petit	5¾ inches	31
Super Hoyos	5½ inches	44
No. 55	5¼ inches	43
Margaritas	5¼ inches	29
Sabrosos	5 inches	40
Rothschild	4½ inches	50
Demitasse	4 inches	39

DOUBLE CORONA : LENGTH 7½ INCHES, RING GAUGE 49

CORONA : LENGTH 5½ INCHES, RING GAUGE 42

MARGARITA : LENGTH 4¾ INCHES, RING GAUGE 26

C Cuba
F Mild
Q Superior quality

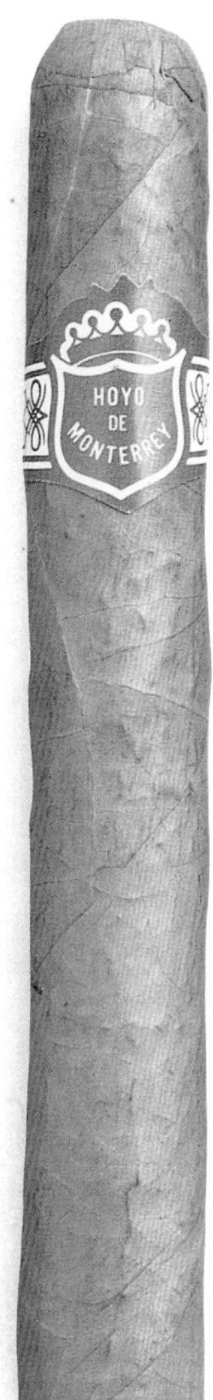

GOVERNOR : LENGTH 6⅛ INCHES, RING GAUGE 50

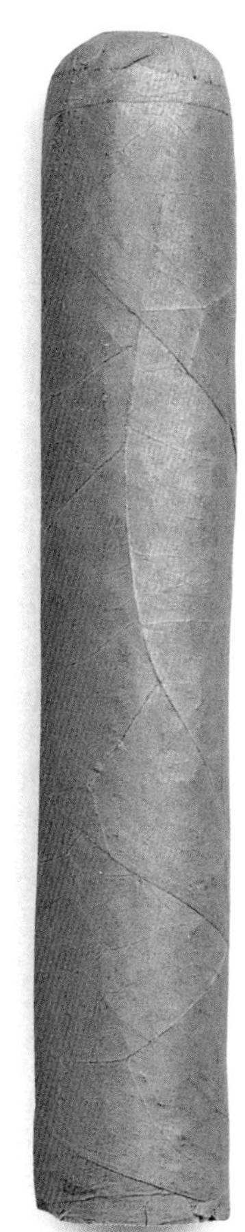

ROTHSCHILD : LENGTH 4½ INCHES, RING GAUGE 50

SULTAN : LENGTH 7¼ INCHES, RING GAUGE 54

C Honduras
F Medium to full-bodied
Q Good-quality leaf and construction

J. R. CIGARS

Lew Rothman is a phenomenon. His J.R. Tobacco of America (J.R. stands for Jack Rothman, Lew's father) covers a mail-order, retail, and wholesale empire that handles 40 percent of all premium cigars sold in the United States.

He built it by playing Robin Hood to the manufacturers' Sheriff of Nottingham. He knows what a cigar costs and won't let his customers pay a cent more than they have to for it. The downside is that some manufacturers like to spend more time and money perfecting cigars to sell at prices Lew won't accept. His sales have rocketed in the cigar boom, so this doesn't seem to matter much. Anyway, no one has to sell to him, and several don't.

If it's the best price you are after, look no further than your nearest J.R. store or catalog where you'll find his own brands of J.R. Ultimate, Special Coronas, and Special Jamaicans.

J. R. ULTIMATE

NAME	LENGTH: INCHES	RING GAUGE
Presidente	8½ inches	52
Super Cetro	8¼ inches	43
No. 1	7¼ inches	54
Cetro	7 inches	42
Slims	6⅞ inches	35
Double Corona	6¾ inches	48
No. 5	6⅛ inches	44
Toro	6 inches	50
Corona	5⅝ inches	46
Petit Corona	4⅝ inches	43
Rothschild	4½ inches	50

C Honduras
F Medium to full-bodied
Q Superior quality

INSIDE J.R.'S CIGAR STORE, THE LARGEST OF ITS KIND IN THE WORLD.

Slims : Length 6⅞ inches, Ring Gauge 35

Petit Corona : Length 4⅝ inches, Ring Gauge 43

Corona : Length 5⅝ inches, Ring Gauge 46

In ascending order of flavor, Special Jamaicans, now made in the Dominican Republic and wrapped in claro Connecticut leaf, are true to their Jamaican origins and as mild as their price. J.R. Special Coronas are also made in the Dominican Republic

SPECIAL CORONAS

NAME	LENGTH: IN/MM	RING GAUGE
Pyramides	7 inches	54
No 754	7 inches	54
No 2	6½ inches	45
No 54	6 inches	54
No 4	5½ inches	45

J. R. TOBACCO OF AMERICA'S LEW ROTHMAN WITH HIS WIFE AND PARTNER LAVONDA.

C Dominican Republic
F Mild to medium
Q Superior quality

from a four-country blend of tobaccos – Ecuadoran wrapper and binder matched with a Brazilian, Honduran, and Dominican filler. They are richer in flavor, but are still mild to medium.

J.R. Ultimate is the flagship. Made in San Pedro Sula, Honduras, from a local blend wrapped in oily Nicaraguan Colorado leaf, they aim to come close to the taste of Havanas. They offer a rich, full-bodied smoke and rate highly among Hondurans.

All these J.R. cigars are very well put together by hand. Whether they are for you depends on how much you mind being seen with the same cigars as so many of the other chaps in Sherwood Forest.

C Dominican Republic
F Mild
Q Superior quality

SPECIAL JAMAICANS

NAME	LENGTH: INCHES	RING GAUGE
Rey del Rey	9 inches	60
Mayfair	7 inches	60
Pyramid	7 inches	52
Churchill	7 inches	52
A	6½ inches	44
D	6 inches	50
B	6 inches	44
C	5½ inches	44
Pica	5 inches	32

CHURCHILL : LENGTH 7IN / 178MM, RING GAUGE 52

JOSE BENITO

These cigars, with their dark Cameroon wrappers, are made in the Dominican Republic. They are well constructed, and generally light to medium-bodied. They all come in attractive varnished cedar boxes (the huge Magnum, 1 inch thick and one of the biggest cigars on the market, is sold in a box by itself), and there are ten sizes.

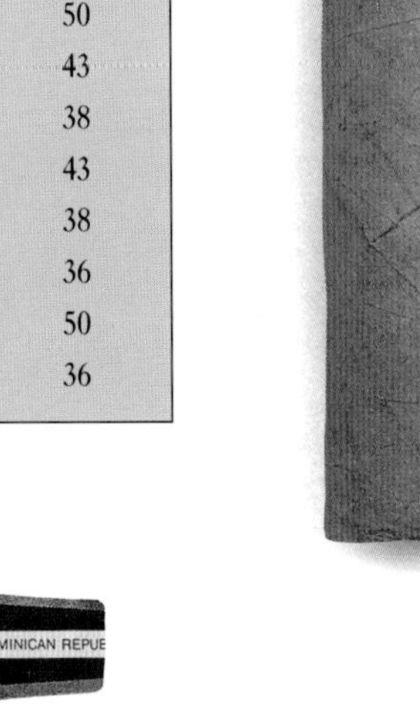

ROTHSCHILD : LENGTH 4½ INCHES, RING GAUGE 50

SIZES

NAME	LENGTH: INCHES	RING GAUGE
Magnum	9 inches	64
Presidente	7¾ inches	50
Churchill	7 inches	50
Corona	6¾ inches	43
Panatela	6¾ inches	38
Palma	6 inches	43
Petite	5½ inches	38
Havanitos	5 inches	36
Rothschild	4½ inches	50
Chico	4 inches	36

C Dominican Republic
F Mild to medium
Q Superior quality

JOYA DE NICARAGUA

Back in the 1970s Nicaraguan cigars were rated by many as the next best to Havanas. The war put an end to that when plantations were laid waste and tobacco barns used to billet Sandinista soldiers.

Since 1990 things have been on the mend, but to re-establish quality in tobacco takes time. The local economy still faces formidable problems, but as every year passes, there is a noticeable improvement in Joya de Nicaragua's standards. Gone is the sweaty aroma of the early 1990's cigars as maturer tobaccos come into use. The more rounded medium flavor with a touch of spice is returning, and the cigars are better constructed and more reliable than they were.

Surprisingly the choice of sizes available in Britain is larger than it is in the United States.

SIZES

NAME	LENGTH: INCHES	RING GAUGE
Viajante	8½ inches	52
Presidente	8 inches	54
Churchill	6⅞ inches	48
No. 5	6⅞ inches	35
No. 10	6½ inches	43
Elegante	6½ inches	38
Corona	5⅝ inches	48
National	5½ inches	44
Seleccion B	5½ inches	42
Petit Corona	5 inches	42
Consul	4½ inches	52
No. 2	4½ inches	41
Piccolino	4⅛ inches	30

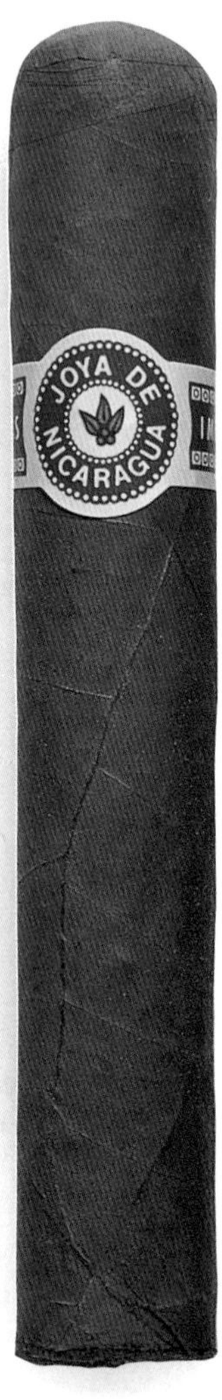

Petit Corona : Length 5 inches, Ring Gauge 42

Elegante : Length 6½ inches, Ring Gauge 38

Presidente : Length 8 inches, Ring Gauge 54

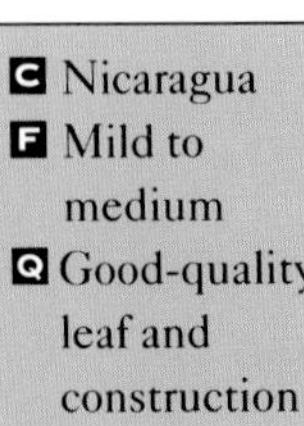

C Nicaragua
F Mild to medium
Q Good-quality leaf and construction

JUAN CLEMENTE

Frenchman Jean Clement hispanicized his name for the Dominican Republic cigar brand he founded in 1982. Wrapped in a claro US Connecticut shade leaf and filled with a blend of Dominican tobacco, it offers a mild, straightforward smoke with a pleasant aroma, best suited to the morning. They have been criticized for their draw, but this seems to be improving. The Club Selection carries a darker wrapper and is well-blended. Uniquely, the band is placed at the foot of the cigar, securing a piece of silver paper which serves to protect its most vulnerable point. Logical, if unconventional.

CLUB SELECTION NO. 2 : LENGTH 4½ INCHES, RING GAUGE 46

SIZES

NAME	LENGTH: INCHES	RING GAUGE
Especiales	7½ inches	38
Club Selection No. 3	7 inches	44
Churchill	6⅞ inches	46
Panetela	6½ inches	34
Club Selection No. 1	6 inches	50
Grand Corona	6 inches	42
Club Selection No. 4	5¾ inches	42
Corona	5 inches	42
No. 530	5 inches	30
Rothschild	4⅞ inches	50
Club Selection No. 2	4½ inches	46
Demi-Corona	4 inches	40

JUAN
CLEMENTE

CLUB SELECTION NO. 3 : LENGTH 7 INCHES, RING GAUGE 44

DEMI CORONA : LENGTH 4 INCHES, RING GAUGE 40

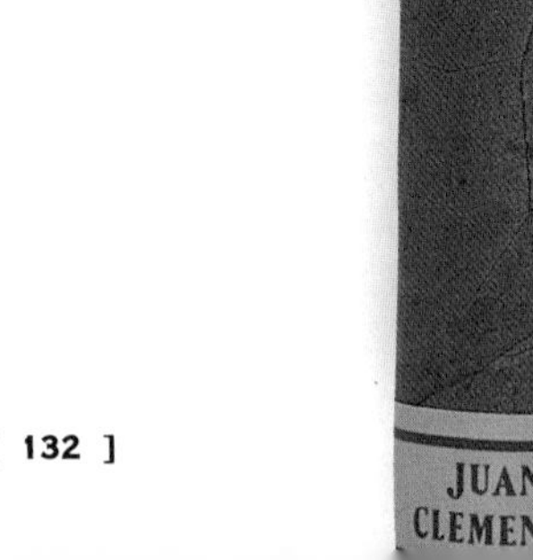

ESPECIALES : LENGTH 7½ INCHES, RING GAUGE 38

C Dominican Republic
F Mild
Q Could be better

Juan Lopez

(Flor de Juan Lopez)

This is an old Havana brand, no longer widely produced or distributed, but is a very light smoke, appealing to some European palates. There are only five sizes. They are fragrant, burn well, and good for daytime smoking. The cigars are really found only in Spain, and the line will soon be reduced to only the Corona and Petit Corona sizes.

SIZES

Name	Length: inches	Ring Gauge
Corona	$5\frac{5}{8}$ inches	42
Petit Coronas	5 inches	42
Placeras	5 inches	34
Slimaranas	$4\frac{3}{4}$ inches	32
Patricias	$4\frac{1}{2}$ inches	40

C Cuba
F Mild
Q Good-quality leaf and construction

SLIMARANAS : LENGTH $4\frac{3}{4}$ INCHES, RING GAUGE 32

LA CORONA

Formerly one of the great Havana brands, although its production was transferred to Trenton, New Jersey, in the 1930s. At present, a small selection of well-made, mild to medium cigars are made in the Dominican Republic by the Consolidated Cigar Corporation. There are also some cigars made in Cuba under this name, but they are either machine-made or hand-finished. The La Corona factory remains in Havana as one of the most important production centers making Punch and Hoyo de Monterrey among others.

SIZES

Name	Length: inches	Ring Gauge
Directors	6½ inches	46
Aristocrats	6⅛ inches	36
Corona	6 1/16 inches	43
Chicas	5½ inches	42

C Dominican Republic
F Mild to medium
Q Good-quality leaf and construction

CORONA : LENGTH 6 1/16 INCHES, RING GAUGE 43

La Flor De Cano

This is a relatively rare Cuban brand, not widely produced or easily available. Rumor has it that Habanos SA has decided to discontinue the handmade sizes like the much-vaunted Short Churchill (a Robusto). Should this prove correct, a group of British fans are considering a campaign to bring them back into production. They are cigars of undoubted quality and interest for those who look for something easy to handle. The Short Churchill, the Punch-Punch sized Gran Corona, and the Diademas are all worth trying, the latter particularly suitable for those who were once Davidoff Dom Perignon fans but don't want to move up to the fuller flavor of the Cohiba Esplendido. Watch out for the many machine-made cigars with names like Preferidos and Selectos that are also available.

C Cuba
F Mild
Q Superior quality

SIZES

Name	Length: inches	Ring Gauge
Diademas	7 inches	47
Corona	5 inches	42
Gran Corona	5⅝ inches	46
Short Churchill	4⅞ inches	50

DIADEMAS : LENGTH 7 INCHES, RING GAUGE 47

La Gloria Cubana

Produced by the Partagas factory, which specializes in full-bodied cigars, this is an old brand which disappeared until it was revived a couple of decades ago to extend the factory's selection of different types of cigar. The Medaille D'Or brand comes in varnished 8–9–8 boxes and the others in labeled boxes.

These are very spicy, rather peppery, strongly aromatic cigars which sometimes fall down (the Lonsdale size, for instance) in construction. They are lighter (more refined, some would say) than the Partagas brand made in the same factory, though still a rich smoke. The line is small, almost all longer sizes.

There is also the Gloria Cubana range made in the United States by Miami's Ernesto Carillo. Ernesto is a man of great integrity whose aim is simply to make the best cigars he can with the best tobaccos he can find. In the main his wrappers are darkish Ecuadoran leaves and his fillers and binders Dominican, Nicaraguan, or Ecuadoran. He blends with his Cuban ancestors in mind to produce full-bodied cigars. The Wavell is strongly recommended if you can find it.

CUBAN SIZES

Name	Length: inches	Ring Gauge
Medaille d'Or 1	7 5/16 inches	36
Tainos	7 inches	47
Medaille d'Or 3	6 7/8 inches	28
Medaille d'Or 2	6 11/16 inches	43
Cetros	6 1/2 inches	42
Sabrosas	6 1/8 inches	42
Medaille d'Or 4	6 inches	32
Tapados	5 5/16 inches	42
Minutos	4 1/2 inches	40

C Cuba
F Medium to full
Q Superior quality

U.S. SIZES

Name	Length: inches	Ring Gauge
Soberano	8 inches	52
Charlemagne	7¼ inches	54
Churchill	7 inches	50
Torpedo	6½ inches	52
Wavell	5 inches	50

C United States
F Medium to full
Q The very best quality available

Medaille d'Or 3 : Length 6⅞ inches, Ring Gauge 28

MEDAILLE D'OR 4 : LENGTH 6 INCHES, RING GAUGE 32

MEDAILLE D'OR 1 : LENGTH $7\frac{5}{16}$ INCHES, RING GAUGE 36

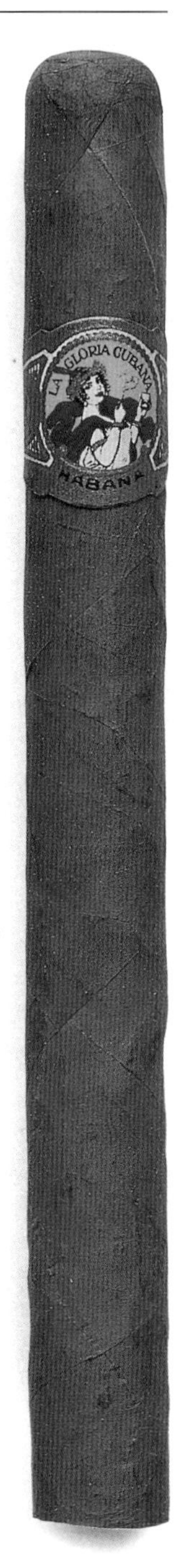

MEDAILLE D'OR 2 : LENGTH $6\frac{11}{16}$ INCHES, RING GAUGE 43

LA INVICTA

These are well-made, medium-bodied Honduran cigars sold mainly in Britain at very reasonable prices in bundles or sometimes in boxes. The wrappers are light to medium in color, with a pleasant bouquet. The cigars draw well, and the flavor is slightly sweet. The aroma is fragrant, and even the smaller sizes are made well enough to remain cool almost to the end. The Gorda (a Rothschild) is a particular favorite.

CHURCHILL : LENGTH 6¾ INCHES, RING GAUGE 47

SIZES

NAME	LENGTH: INCHES	RING GAUGE
Especiales	6⅞ inches	36
Churchill	6¾ inches	47
Corona	5½ inches	42
Panetela	5¼ inches	26
Petit Corona	5 inches	42
Gordas	4½ inches	50

C Honduras
F Medium to full
Q Good-quality leaf and construction

LICENCIADOS

On the market since 1990, the makers of Licenciados chose to take the Disneyesque carriage and scrolls design found on Havana's Diplomaticos brand as their emblem. Blends of Dominican fillers are dressed in light Connecticut shade wrappers for the main range, while Connecticut broadleaf is used for a smaller maduro series, known as Supreme. The Robusto-sized Wavell comes in both wrapper colors. These are classic, mild, Connecticut Dominican Republic cigars, well-made and competitively priced.

PANETELA : LENGTH 7 INCHES, RING GAUGE 38

SIZES

NAME	LENGTH: INCHES	RING GAUGE
Soberano	8½ inches	52
Presidente	8 inches	50
Panetela	7 inches	38
Excelente	6¾ inches	43
Toro	6 inches	50
Licenciados No. 4	5¾ inches	43
Wavell	5 inches	50
SUPREME RANGE		
500	8 inches	50
300	6¾ inches	43
400	6 inches	50
200	5¾ inches	43

C Dominican Republic
F Mild
Q Superior quality

MACANUDO

This brand, founded in Jamaica in 1868, is now made by General Cigar in both Jamaica and the Dominican Republic, under the supervision of Benjamin Menendez. The blend is the same for both countries of origin: Connecticut Shade wrapper, binder from the San Andres area of Mexico, and a mixture of Jamaican, Mexican, and Dominican tobacco for the filler.

These are undoubtedly handsome, consistently very well-made cigars, which provide one of the very best smooth, mild smokes on the market. The word *macanudo* means fine, dandy, or a good thing in colloquial Spanish and, for once in a cigar name, is pretty near the truth.

There is a wide variety of sizes, some of which (mostly larger ring gauges) come in a choice of wrapper color: café (made with Connecticut Shade wrapper), the even milder jade (a greenish, double claro wrapper), and the fuller and nutty-sweet maduro (in which case, the deep brown wrapper comes from Mexico). The Hampton Court and Portofino sizes come in elegant white aluminum tubes. The Claybourne and Prince Philip sizes are made in the Dominican Republic, the others (normally) in Jamaica. Macanudos don't come cheap; the Connecticut wrapper sees to that. They normally come wrapped in cellophane. If there's one criticism, it's that they are somewhat short on aroma, but they are an excellent daytime smoke, or suitable after a light meal. The fuller-bodied Macanudo Vintage cigars are sold at much higher prices and designed for the connoisseur. They are all made in Jamaica, with Dominican filler.

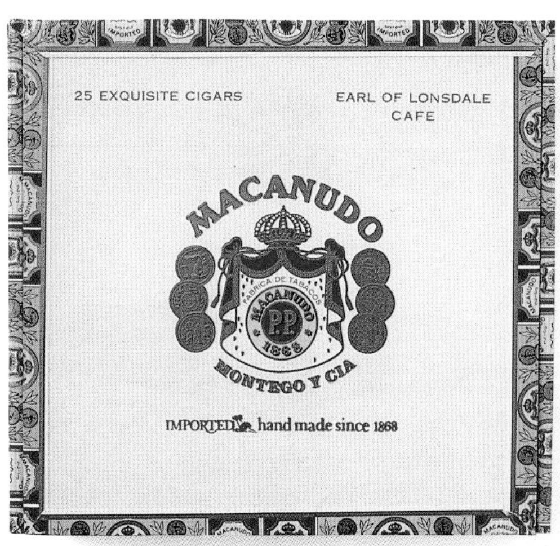

SIZES

NAME	LENGTH: INCHES	RING GAUGE
Duke of Wellington	$8\frac{1}{2}$ inches	38
Prince Philip	$7\frac{1}{2}$ inches	49
Vintage No. I	$7\frac{1}{2}$ inches	49
Sovereign	7 inches	45
Somerset	7 inches	34
Portofino	7 inches	34
Earl of Lonsdale	$6\frac{3}{4}$ inches	38
Vintage No. II	$6\frac{9}{16}$ inches	43
Baron de Rothschild	$6\frac{1}{2}$ inches	42
Amatista	$6\frac{1}{4}$ inches	42
Claybourne	6 inches	31
Hampton Court	$5\frac{3}{4}$ inches	43
Vintage No. III	$5\frac{9}{16}$ inches	43
Hyde Park	$5\frac{1}{2}$ inches	49
Duke of Devon	$5\frac{1}{2}$ inches	42
Lord Claridge	$5\frac{1}{2}$ inches	38
Quill	$5\frac{1}{4}$ inches	28
Petit Corona	5 inches	38
Vintage No. IV	$4\frac{1}{2}$ inches	47
Ascot	$4\frac{3}{16}$ inches	32
Caviar	4 inches	36

VINTAGE NO. 1 : LENGTH $7\frac{1}{2}$ INCHES, RING GAUGE 49

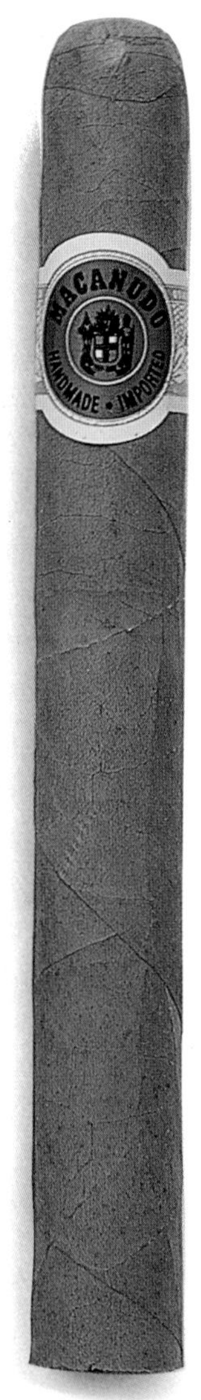

DUKE OF DEVON : LENGTH $5\frac{1}{2}$ INCHES, RING GAUGE 42

CLAYBOURNE : LENGTH 6 INCHES, RING GAUGE 31

C Jamaica
F Mild
Q Superior quality

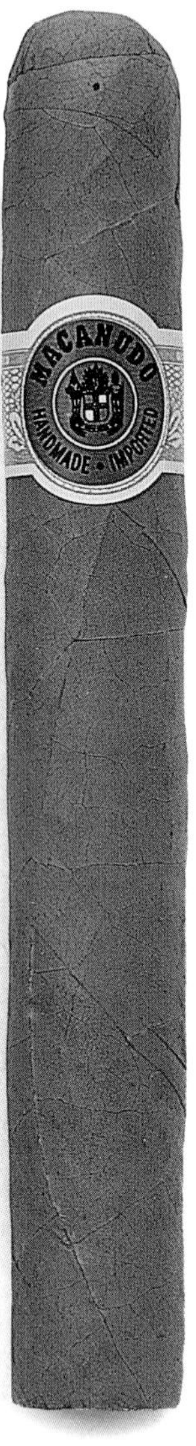

HYDE PARK : LENGTH 5½ INCHES, RING GAUGE 49

PORTOFINO : LENGTH 7 INCHES, RING GAUGE 34

PRINCE PHILIP : LENGTH 7½ INCHES, RING GAUGE 49

C Dominican Republic
F Mild
Q Superior quality

MATACAN

A minor brand from Mexico, made by the Consolidated Cigar Corporation, also responsible for the Te-Amo brand, in the San Andres Valley. They come in light brown and maduro wrappers. They are well made, less tightly rolled than Te-Amo (though they have similar coarse wrappers), draw well, and have a spicy, slightly sweet, if nonetheless rather bland, medium to full flavor. All things considered, they are somewhat superior to Te-Amo, even though they are cheaper. Try the No. 7.

SIZES

NAME	LENGTH: INCHES	RING GAUGE
No. 8	8 inches	52
No. 1	7½ inches	50
No. 3	6⅝ inches	46
No. 4	6⅝ inches	42
No. 6	6⅝ inches	35
No. 2	6 inches	50
No. 5	6 inches	42
No. 9	5 inches	32
No. 7	4¾ inches	50

C Mexico
F Medium to full-bodied
Q Good-quality leaf and construction

NO. 8 : LENGTH 8 INCHES, RING GAUGE 52

Mocha Supreme

These are handmade cigars from Honduras, using Havana seed wrappers. They are well-constructed and, for a boxed cigar, well-priced. Generally they are medium to full-bodied in flavor, but noticeably milder than many Hondurans. There is a woody, nutty hint to their taste.

SIZES

Name	Length: inches	Ring Gauge
Rembrandt	8½ inches	52
Patron	7½ inches	50
Lords	6½ inches	42
Allegro	6½ inches	36
Renaissance	6 inches	50
Sovereign	5½ inches	42
Baron de Rothschild	4½ inches	52
Petites	4½ inches	42

Allegro : Length 6½ inches, Ring Gauge 36

PETITES : LENGTH 4½ INCHES, RING GAUGE 42

PATRON : LENGTH 7½ INCHES, RING GAUGE 50

BARON DE ROTHSCHILD : LENGTH 4½ INCHES, RING GAUGE 52

C Honduras
F Medium to full-bodied
Q Good-quality leaf and construction

MONTECRISTO

Montecristo is the most popular Havana by far. Around half of the cigars exported from Cuba in any one year bear its simple brown and white band.

Ironically, perhaps, it started life in 1935 as a brand limited to just five sizes which its founders, Alonzo Menendez and Pepe Garcia, aimed to keep in restricted distribution. They had just bought the H. Upmann brand from the British firm J. Frankau, and their main task was to extend its volume. Montecristo, first known as H. Upmann Montecristo Selection and sold through Dunhill in New York, was a prestigious sideline to test Menendez's leaf skills and Garcia's knowledge of production.

The change of name simply to Montecristo was inspired by another British firm, John Hunter, which was appointed as the British agent. The rival company Frankau handled Upmann and wanted Montecristo to stand on its own. The outstanding red and yellow box design with its triangular crossed swords is attributed to the Hunter company.

World War II interrupted the flow of Havanas to Britain, so the brand's development was concentrated in the United States, mainly through Dunhill's stores. Film director Alfred Hitchcock was an early devotee and regularly sent supplies back to friends deprived by wartime restrictions in England.

After the war the Tubos size was added, but otherwise the line remained the same.

Shortly after Castro came to power, the Menendez and Garcia families moved to the Canary Islands. Some continuity was provided by a legendary figure who remained on the home island. He was Jose Manuel Gonzalez, known as "Masinguila." Considered in Havana to this day as the finest cigar maker ever and one of the hardest taskmasters for the rollers he supervised, "Masinguila" is generally credited with much of the consistency in quality and unique blending that is characteristic of the brand.

In the early 1970s, the Montecristo A and the Laguito (Cohiba) Nos. 1, 2, and 3 sizes were added as the Especial, Especial No. 2, and Joyita. Coincidentally, the brand took off. It became the firm showbiz favorite with the likes of singer Tom Jones and British movie mogul Lew (now Lord) Grade.

Some say success brought its own problems. Certainly to match the quality of the huge volume of Montecristos that go to Spain, for example, is a prodigious task, and many consider that higher standards are maintained only in smaller markets like Britain. However, this did not stop an outbreak of near civil unrest in Spain when the brand was withdrawn following a trademark dispute between Tabacalera (the Spanish monopoly) and Cubatabaco.

The signs are that the trademark issue has been resolved, at least in Spain if not in France. However, this has no bearing on the introduction of a line of Dominican Montecristos in the United States.

Montecristos, with their characteristic Colorado-claro, slightly oily wrappers and delicate aroma offer a medium to full flavor spiked with a unique, tangy taste. The No. 2 is the flagship for the Piramide size, while many devotees consider the No. 1 (a Cervantes) hard to beat.

MONTECRISTO

SIZES

NAME	LENGTH: INCHES	RING GAUGE
A	9¼ inches	47
Especial	7½ inches	38
No. 1	6½ inches	42
No. 2	6⅛ inches	52
Especial No. 2	6 inches	38
Tubos	6 inches	42
No. 3	5½ inches	42
Petit Tubos	5 inches	42
No. 4	5 inches	42
Joyitas	4½ inches	26
No. 5	4 inches	40

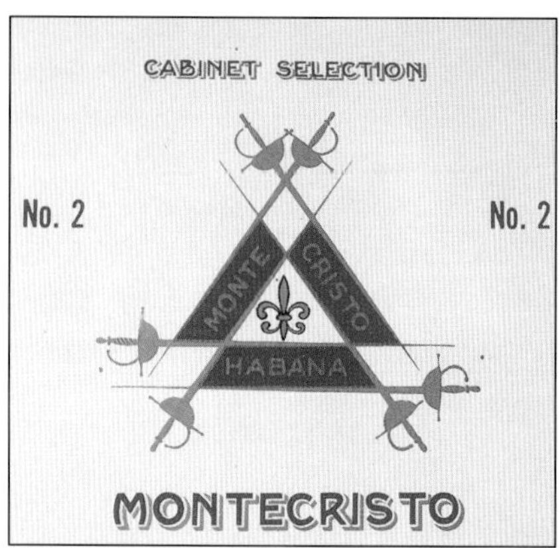

ESPECIAL NO. 2 : LENGTH 6 INCHES, RING GAUGE 38

NO. 2 : LENGTH 6⅛ INCHES, RING GAUGE 52

TUBOS : LENGTH 6 INCHES, RING GAUGE 42

NO. 5 : LENGTH 4 INCHES, RING GAUGE 40

- **C** Cuba
- **F** Medium to full-bodied
- **Q** Superior quality

MONTECRUZ

Montecruz was the brand name given to the cigars made by the Menendez family (former owners of the Montecristo brand) when they started a manufacturing operation in the Canary Islands after leaving Cuba. They were then made with Cameroon wrappers, with Dominican and Brazilian fillers. The cigars, with labels very similar to the Montecristo brand are now made (since the mid-1970s) at La Romana in the Dominican Republic, with mid- to dark-brown Cameroon wrappers, by the Consolidated Cigar Corporation. These very well-made, medium to full-flavored cigars (with a distinctive taste and bouquet) come in a very wide choice of sizes. They are described as "sun grown." The "boîte nature" selection is richer, and matured for longer. Montecruz cigars are also produced in a milder range (with different labels and lighter Connecticut wrappers) for Dunhill. The Dunhill cigars come in some of the same sizes as the Montecruz.

SIZES

NAME	LENGTH: INCHES	RING GAUGE
Indivuales	8 inches	50
Montecruz F	7¼ inches	47
No. 200	7¼ inches	46
No. 205	7 inches	42
No. 255	7 inches	36
Montecruz D	7 inches	36
No. 280	7 inches	33
Montecruz A	6⅝ inches	43
Colossus	6½ inches	50
No. 210	6½ inches	42
No. 250	6½ inches	38
No. 201	6⅛ inches	38
No. 281	6 inches	33
Montecruz C	5⅝ inches	43
No. 220	5½ inches	42
No. 265	5½ inches	38
No. 282	5 inches	42
Cedar-aged	5 inches	42
Numero 333	5 inches	33
Juniors	4⅞ inches	33
No. 240	4¾ inches	44
No. 270	4¾ inches	35
Chicos	3⅞ inches	28

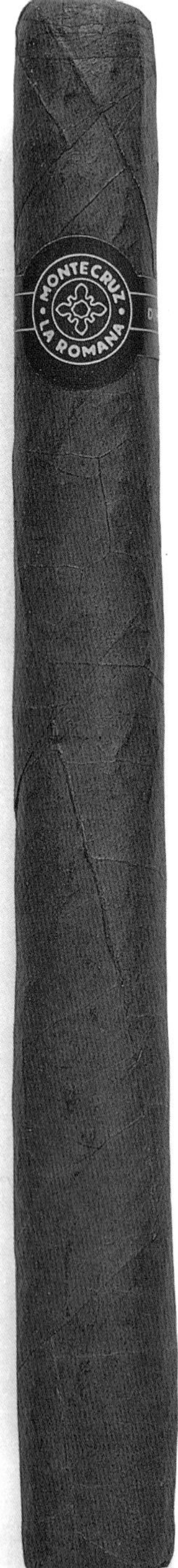

No. 200 : Length 7¼ inches, Ring Gauge 46

No. 210 : Length 6½ inches, Ring Gauge 42

No. 282 : Length 5 inches, Ring Gauge 42

C Dominican Republic
F Medium to full-bodied
Q Superior quality

No. 255 : Length 7 inches, Ring Gauge 36

Tube Dunhill Sun Grown

Colossus : Length 6½ inches, Ring Gauge 50

MONTESINO

A medium-bodied brand made in Dominican Republic by Arturo Fuente with Havana Fuente seed wrappers, which are mid-brown to dark. These cigars are well made and reasonably priced for the quality.

SIZES

Name	Length: inches	Ring Gauge
Napoleon Grande	7 inches	46
No. 1	6⅞ inches	43
Fumas	6¾ inches	44
No. 3	6¾ inches	36
Gran Corona	6¾ inches	48
No. 2	6¼ inches	44
Diplomatico	5½ inches	42

C Dominican Republic
F Mild to medium
Q Good-quality leaf and construction

GRAN CORONA : LENGTH 6¾ INCHES, RING GAUGE 48

NAT SHERMAN

The Nat Sherman store at 500 Fifth Avenue is a polished mahogany temple to tobacco, cigars, and smokers' requisites. Its business, which stretches far beyond its doors, was founded in New York's heyday of the 1930s and 40s with stylish cigarettes and strong connections in Havana.

Joel Sherman, its present custodian, anticipated the cigar boom back in 1990 and 1991, introducing four cigar selections, all made in the Dominican Republic but each with a different blend.

There is the Exchange Selection, named after New York's 1940s telephone exchanges, including the inevitable Butterfield 8 (a Lonsdale). Four different countries supply the blend of leaves for these cigars including the lightest of Connecticut wrappers. The flavor is mild.

Dressed in Cameroon wrappers, the Landmark Selection (Metropole, Algonquin, etc.) offers another four-country confection with a bit more flavor and a chocolaty top taste.

THE FINE EXTERIOR OF THE NAT SHERMAN SHOP IN NEW YORK.

Cigar-chomping editors of New York's former newspapers are commemorated by the four hefty, sweet-tasting Mexican maduro sizes in the City Desk Selection. Their mild to medium flavor belies their looks.

On the other hand, the Gotham Selection wrapped in a mid-tone Connecticut leaf delivers a surprisingly spicy, yet well balanced, taste.

Each series is identified by a different background color to the emblem of a clock on the band. Go for gray; go for Gotham.

C Dominican Republic
F Varies according to selection
Q Superior quality

GOTHAM 500 : LENGTH 7 INCHES, RING GAUGE 50

SIZES

NAME	LENGTH: INCHES	RING GAUGE
GOTHAM SELECTION		
500	7 inches	50
1400	6¼ inches	44
711	6 inches	50
65	6 inches	36
CITY DESK SELECTION		
Tribune	7½ inches	50
Dispatch	6½ inches	46
Telegraph	6 inches	50
Gazette	6 inches	42
LANDMARK SELECTION		
Dakota	7½ inches	49
Algonquin	6¾ inches	43
Metropole	6 inches	34
Hampshire	5½ inches	42
Vanderbilt	5 inches	47
EXCHANGE SELECTION		
Oxford 5	7 inches	49
Butterfield 8	6½ inches	42
Trafalgar 4	6 inches	47
Murray 7	6 inches	38
Academy 2	5 inches	31

GOTHAM 1400 : LENGTH 6¼ INCHES, RING GAUGE 44

CITY DESK TELEGRAPH : LENGTH 6 INCHES, RING GAUGE 50

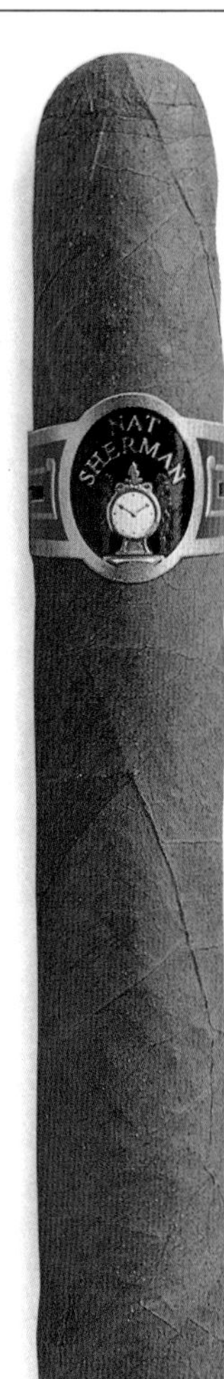

LANDMARK VANDERBILT : LENGTH 5 INCHES, RING GAUGE 47

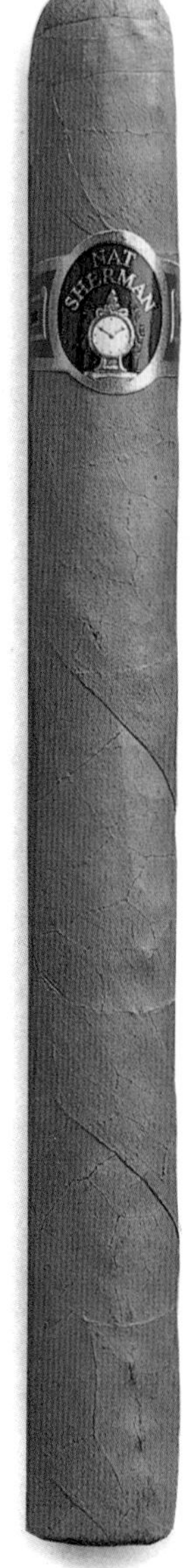

EXCHANGE MURRAY 7 : LENGTH 6 INCHES, RING GAUGE 38

OSCAR

These Dominican Republic cigars, named after the company's founder, are well-filled and elegantly presented in claro U.S. Connecticut wrappers. The fillers and binders form a mild to medium blend made from locally produced tobaccos. They have been on the market for nearly a decade and have benefitted from the general improvement in the quality of Dominican cigars. The line covers most needs, including a couple of useful smaller sizes alongside some giants.

#500 : LENGTH 5½ INCHES, RING GAUGE 50

SIZES

NAME	LENGTH: INCHES	RING GAUGE
Don Oscar	9 inches	46
Supreme	8 inches	48
#700	7 inches	54
#200	7 inches	44
#100	7 inches	38
#300	6¼ inches	44
#400	6 inches	38
#500	5½ inches	50
Prince	5 inches	30
#600	4½ inches	50
Oscarito	4 inches	20

C Dominican Republic
F Mild to medium
Q Good-quality and leaf construction

PARTAGAS

Partagas is one of the oldest of the Havana brands, started in 1845 by Don Jaime Partagas. The old factory still exists, in downtown Havana near the Capitol building (an architectural copy of the United States Congress). The name is still well known, not least because Partagas cigars are produced in large quantities: there are no fewer than 40 types available – many of them machine-made and cellophane-wrapped. There is also a Dominican version of the brand, made with Cameroon wrappers grown from Havana seed, and overseen by Benjamin Menendez and Ramon Cifuentes of the famous Cuban cigar families. The brand is manufactured by General Cigar. The differences between the labels are that Cuban versions carry the word Habana at the bottom of the label, whereas Dominican versions have the year 1845.

The brand was particularly famous between the two World Wars and has the distinction of being mentioned in cigar-lover Evelyn Waugh's novel, *Brideshead Revisited.*

The quality of Cuban Partagas can vary. The bigger sizes like the Lusitania, particularly in Cabinet 50's (a firm favorite with ABC's Pierre Salinger) are very good indeed, but some of the

CUBAN SIZES

Name	Length: inches	Ring Gauge
Lusitanias	7⅝ inches	49
Churchill De Luxe	7 inches	47
Palmes Grandes	7 inches	33
Partagas de Partagas No. 1	6¹¹⁄₁₆ inches	43
Seleccion Privada No. 1	6¹¹⁄₁₆ inches	43
8-9-8	6¹¹⁄₁₆ inches	43
Lonsdale	6½ inches	42
Corona Grande	6 inches	42
Culebras (twisted)	5¹¹⁄₁₆ inches	39
Corona	5½ inches	42
Charlotte	5½ inches	35
Petit Corona	5 inches	42
Series D No. 4	4⅞ inches	50
Très Petit Corona	4½ inches	40
Shorts	4⁵⁄₁₆ inches	42

smaller sizes, often when they are machine-made as opposed to hand-finished or handmade, can give draw problems. In general, the brand has a rich, earthy, and full flavor, which is particularly noticeable on the heavier ring gauge sizes like the Series D No. 4 (Robusto). There are two sizes in an 8–9–8 packing; one is a Corona Grande (6 inches × 42) and the other a Dalia (6⅝ inches × 43). The Dalia is seen by Ernesto Lopez, the factory's Director, as his flagship size. They have an altogether smoother finish, but retain the full flavor. There is a Connoisseur series of three cigars, available in some markets, which includes the No. 1, a cigar of the same dimensions as the Cohiba Lanceros but without the pigtail. In general, Partagas is a good choice after a heavy meal.

Handmade Dominican Partagas, although very well-constructed, occasionally have wrappers of variable quality, particularly the larger sizes. The best are very good. They are also relatively expensive. They normally come in colorado wrappers, but there is also a maduro – a 6¼-inch cigar with a 47 ring gauge. The fillers are a mixture of Jamaican, Dominican, and Mexican tobacco. There are 14 sizes, mostly numbered, of Dominican Partagas in all: smooth, medium to full-bodied, and slightly sweet. A selection of sizes is listed.

ERNESTO LOPEZ, DIRECTOR OF THE PARTAGAS FACTORY IN DOWNTOWN HAVANA.

SERIES D NO. 4: LENGTH $4\frac{7}{8}$ INCHES, RING GAUGE 50

CORONA : LENGTH $5\frac{1}{2}$ INCHES, RING GAUGE 42

SHORTS : LENGTH $4\frac{5}{16}$ INCHES, RING GAUGE 42

C Cuba
F Very full-bodied
Q Superior quality

DOMINICAN SIZES

Name	Length: inches	Ring Gauge
No. 10	7½ inches	49
8–9–8	6 13/16 inches	44
Limited Reserve Royale	6¾ inches	43
No. 1	6 11/16 inches	43
Limited Reserve Regale	6¼ inches	47
Maduro	6¼ inches	47
No. 6	6 inches	34
No. 5	5¼ inches	28
Purito	4 3/16 inches	32

C Dominican Republic
F Medium to full-bodied
Q Superior quality

LIMITED RESERVE ROYALE : LENGTH 6¾ INCHES, RING GAUGE 43

Paul Garmirian

Paul Garmirian's P.G. cigars are among the best on the market – certainly when it comes to non-Havanas. Garmirian himself, based outside Washington, DC, has a Ph.D. in international politics and is a real-estate broker. He is also a great connoisseur of handmade cigars, and author of *The Gourmet Guide to Cigars*. He decided to put his 30-year passion for fine cigars to work in 1991 with the launch of his own brand.

His cigars, available only in limited quantities, are made in the Dominican Republic with dark, slightly oily, reddish mid-brown colorado wrappers. They are very well made, have a subtle but noticeable bouquet, burn well and slowly, and are medium flavored. The cigars have a rich aroma, taste pleasantly sweet (the flavor gets richer as you smoke), and are very mellow and well blended. These are very superior cigars, as good as many Havanas, and better than quite a few. The Lonsdale will give you a pretty good impression of the line, to which five more sizes have been added since the first edition of this book. There is a 7-inch, 52 ring gauge Magnum out soon, which is worth waiting for.

CORONA : LENGTH 5½ INCHES, RING GAUGE 42

C Dominican Republic
F Medium to full-bodied
Q Superior quality

SIZES

NAME	LENGTH: INCHES	RING GAUGE
Celebration	9 inches	50
Double Corona	7⅝ inches	50
Magnum	7 inches	52
Churchill	7 inches	48
Belicoso	6½ inches	52
Corona Grande	6½ inches	46
Lonsdale	6½ inches	42
No. 1	6½ inches	38
Connoisseur	6 inches	50
Belicoso Fino	5½ inches	52
Epicure	5½ inches	50
Corona	5½ inches	42
Robusto	5 inches	50
Petit Corona	5 inches	43
No. 2	4¾ inches	48
Petit Bouquet	4½ inches	38
No. 5	4 inches	40

CHURCHILL : LENGTH 7 INCHES, RING GAUGE 48

NO. 2 : LENGTH 4¾ INCHES, RING GAUGE 48

BELICOSO : LENGTH 6½ INCHES, RING GAUGE 52

CELEBRATION : LENGTH 9 INCHES, RING GAUGE 50

PLEIADES

A very elegant range of Dominican cigars with Connecticut Shade wrappers. They are mild, well made, draw well, and are very pleasant cigars with a good aroma. The brand originates from France. Once made in the Caribbean, the cigars are shipped back to Strasbourg, where they are placed in boxes with an original built-in humidifying system, before being distributed in Europe and back across the ocean to the United States.

URANUS : LENGTH 6⅞ INCHES, RING GAUGE 34

SIZES

NAME	LENGTH: INCHES	RING GAUGE
Aldebran	8½ inches	50
Saturne	8 inches	46
Neptune	7½ inches	42
Sirius	6⅞ inches	46
Uranus	6⅞ inches	34
Orion	5¾ inches	42
Antares	5½ inches	40
Pluton	5 inches	50
Perseus	5 inches	34
Mars	5 inches	28

C Dominican Republic
F Mild
Q Good-quality leaf and construction

ORION : LENGTH $5\frac{3}{4}$ INCHES, RING GAUGE 42

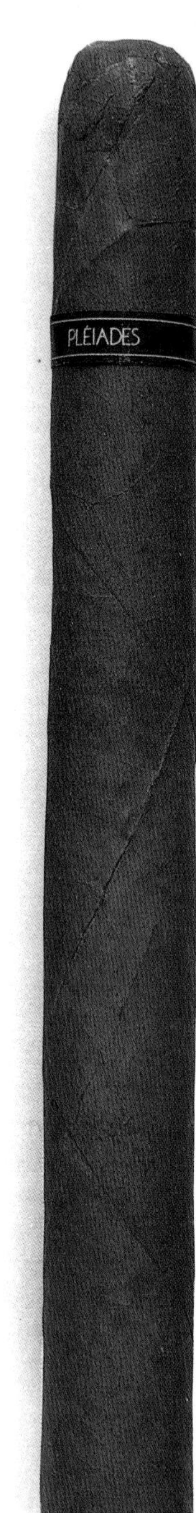

SIRIUS : LENGTH $6\frac{7}{8}$ INCHES, RING GAUGE 46

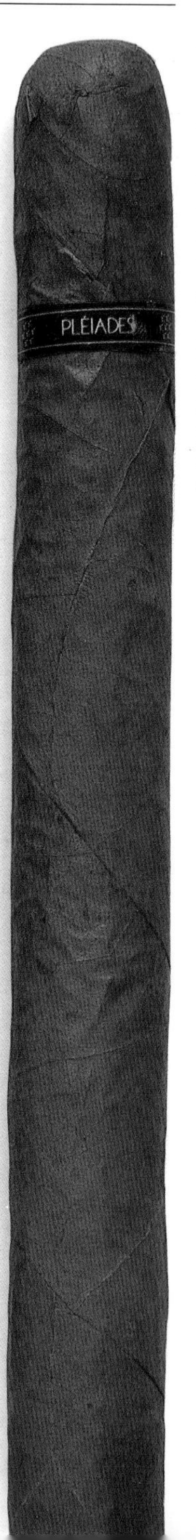

ALDEBRAN : LENGTH $8\frac{1}{2}$ INCHES, RING GAUGE 50

POR LARRANAGA

An old brand (the oldest still being produced), dating from 1834, but no longer among the best known. Production is limited, and the cigars aren't widely distributed, but these very full-bodied cigars are sought after by many connoisseurs of traditional Havana flavor. The selection is fairly limited, with about half a dozen machine-made sizes (the brand was the first to introduce machines), some the same (size, not quality) as handmade versions. "There's peace in Larranaga," claimed Rudyard Kipling in his 1890 ditty which includes the notorious line "A woman is only a woman, but a good cigar is a smoke."

These cigars, with their dark, reddish, oily wrappers, are a good choice for lovers of mid- to full-flavored cigars. With their golden bands, they have a distinguished appearance. They tend to be rich and aromatic, with a powerful (rather sweet) flavor, and an aroma less pronounced than some other brands of the same type (Partagas, for instance). The Lonsdale and Corona sizes are as good as most rivals, and the latter is a good after-dinner cigar.

There are also excellent Dominican cigars using the same brand name. They are extremely well made with Connecticut Shade wrappers, fillers blended from Dominican and Brazilian leaves, and Dominican binders. They are full of flavor, especially the Fabuloso (7 inches, ring gauge 50), which is essentially a Churchill.

CUBAN SIZES

NAME	LENGTH: INCHES	RING GAUGE
Lonsdale	6½ inches	42
Corona	5½ inches	42
Petit Corona	5 inches	42
Small Corona	4½ inches	40

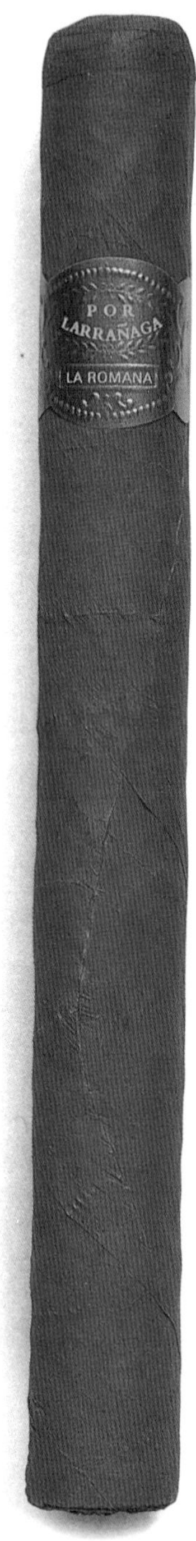

Fabuloso : Length 7 inches, Ring Gauge 50

Robostos : Length 5 inches, Ring Gauge 50

- **C** Dominican Republic
- **F** Mild to medium
- **Q** Superior quality

Corona : Length $5\frac{1}{2}$ inches, Ring Gauge 42

- **C** Cuba
- **F** Medium to full-bodied
- **Q** Superior quality

PRIMO DEL REY

A brand made by the Consolidated Cigar Corporation in the Dominican Republic. The main line consisting of 1–5 sizes dressed in a simple brown and white Montecristo-like band, offers a choice of Candela (double claro), Claro (natural), and Colorado (mid-brown wrappers). Just four sizes make up the Club Selection, which is identified by a red, gold, and white band featuring a coat of arms. They are all very well-made.

SIZES

NAME	LENGTH: INCHES	RING GAUGE
Barons	8½ inches	52
Aguillas	8 inches	52
Soberanos	7½ inches	50
Regal	7 inches	50
Aristocrats	6¹³⁄₁₆ inches	48
Presidentes	6¹³⁄₁₆ inches	44
Seleccion No. 1	6¹³⁄₁₆ inches	42
Seleccion No. 3	6¹³⁄₁₆ inches	36
Chavon	6½ inches	41
Churchill	6½ inches	41
Nobles	6⁵⁄₁₆ inches	44
Seleccion No. 2	6¼ inches	42
Cazadores	6⅛ inches	42
Reales	6⅛ inches	36
Almirantes	6 inches	50
Panetela Extra	5⁵⁄₁₆ inches	34
Panetela	5⁵⁄₁₆ inches	34
Seleccion No. 4	5½ inches	42
No. 100	4½ inches	50

REGAL : LENGTH 7 INCHES, RING GAUGE 50

SOBERANOS : LENGTH 7½ INCHES, RING GAUGE 50

NO. 100 : LENGTH 4½ INCHES, RING GAUGE 50

ALMIRANTES : LENGTH 6 INCHES, RING GAUGE 50

C Dominican Republic
F Mild to medium
Q Superior quality

ARISTOCRATS : LENGTH $6\frac{13}{16}$ INCHES, RING GAUGE 48

NOBLES : LENGTH $6\frac{5}{16}$ INCHES, RING GAUGE 44

BARONS : LENGTH $8\frac{1}{2}$ INCHES, RING GAUGE 52

PUNCH

A very well-known and widely distributed Havana brand (once very popular in Britain), with lower prices than many others, and as a result, familiar to beginners and occasional smokers. Cigar snobs thus tend to avoid it, mostly without good reason. There is a very wide selection of sizes, mostly from the La Corona factory, with many machine-made equivalents – as well as types such as Exquisitos and Palmas Reales, which are only machine-made.

The brand, the second oldest still in production, was founded in 1840 by Manuel Lopez with the British market in mind where an eponymous light-hearted magazine (similar to the New Yorker) was much in vogue. A contented Mr. Punch, cigar in hand, remains a feature of each box.

There is also a Honduran Punch brand which comes in three series; standard, Delux, and Gran Cru. These are exceptionally well-made cigars, particularly in the Delux and Gran Cru form. The standard line offers a straightforward, Honduran, fullish flavor, but there is a rare delicacy to the taste in the other two series, even

CUBAN SIZES

NAME	LENGTH: INCHES	RING GAUGE
Diademas Extra	9¼ inches	47
Double Corona	7⅝ inches	49
Churchill	7 inches	47
Corona	5⅝ inches	42
Punch Punch	5½ inches	46
Royal Coronations	5½ inches	42
Petit Corona	5 inches	42
Coronations	5 inches	42
Margarita	4¾ inches	26
Coronets	4½ inches	40
Punchinellos	4½ inches	34
Très Petit Coronas	4¼ inches	42
Petit Punch	4 inches	40

when maduro wrapped, which suggests substantial aging. The skilled hands and expert knowledge of Villazon's Frank Llaneza lie behind these cigars, which is always a good sign.

With such a large Havana line, it isn't possible for every cigar to be of the highest quality, but the larger sizes, with their fragrant bouquet, distinctive spicy aroma, and reasonably, but not very, full-bodied, slightly sweet flavor, are well-constructed and dependable – the Double Corona, for instance. One complication is that the same-sized cigars are sometimes known by different names in different countries. The famous Punch Punch (Corona Gorda), for example, can be found as a Royal Selection No. 11 or a Seleccion de Luxe No. 1, and even the Petit Corona del Punch is sometimes the Seleccion de Luxe No. 2 or Presidente. Find a trusty cigar merchant to guide you through this choice of first class mild to medium cigars.

There are tubed cigars in both the Cuban and Honduran lines, with names like Royal Coronation.

HONDURAN SIZES

Name	Length: inches	Ring Gauge
Presidente	8½ inches	42
Château Lafitte	7¼ inches	52
Grand Diademas	7⅛ inches	52
Diademas	7⅛ inches	52
Elegante	7⅛ inches	36
Casa Grande	7 inches	46
Monarcas	6¾ inches	48
Double Corona	6⅝ inches	48
Château Corona	6½ inches	44
No. 1	6½ inches	42
Bristol	6¼ inches	50
Britania Delux	6¼ inches	50
Punch	6⅛ inches	43
Superiores Delux	5⅝ inches	46
Château Margaux	5½ inches	46
No. 75	5½ inches	43
Superior	5 inches	50
Rothschild	4½ inches	48

C Honduras
F Mild to medium
Q Superior quality

DOUBLE CORONA : LENGTH 7⅝ INCHES, RING GAUGE 49

PETIT CORONA : LENGTH 5 INCHES, RING GAUGE 42

PUNCH PUNCH : LENGTH 5½ INCHES, RING GAUGE 46

C Cuba
F Mild to medium
Q Superior quality

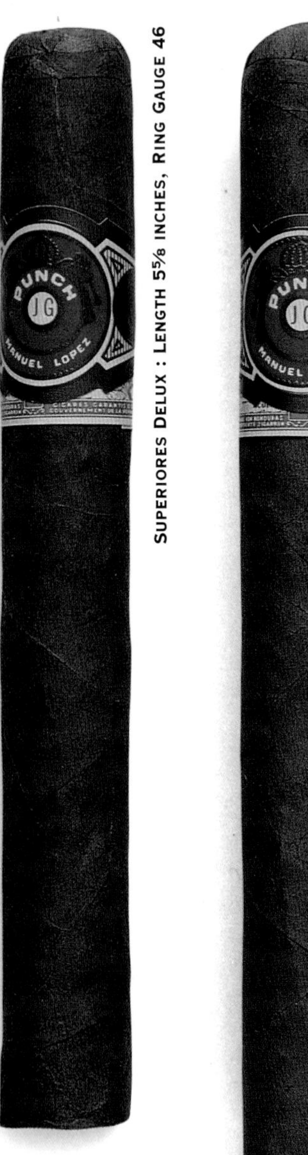

SUPERIORES DELUX : LENGTH 5⅝ INCHES, RING GAUGE 46

BRITANIA DELUX : LENGTH 6¼ INCHES, RING GAUGE 50

MONARCAS : LENGTH 6¾ INCHES, RING GAUGE 48

QUINTERO

A Cuban brand notable for the fact that it was founded in the southern coastal city of Cienfuegos, and not Havana. Augustin Quintero and his four brothers, who worked in the nearby Remedios tobacco regime, started a small "chinchal" (cigar workshop) in the mid-1920s. By 1940, their reputation allowed them to open in Havana and introduce the brand bearing their family name using Vuelta Abajo tobaccos. Today several of the sizes are both handmade or machine-made, so check for the "Totalamente a mano" stamp on the box. The Churchill is a Lonsdale (Cervantes), but a good one if you like a light smoke. Overall the brand is mild.

PANETELA : LENGTH 5 INCHES, RING GAUGE 37

SIZES

NAME	LENGTH: INCHES	RING GAUGE
Churchill	6½ inches	42
Corona	5½ inches	42
Nacionales	5½ inches	40
Panetelas	5 inches	37
Tubulares	5 inches	37
Londres Extra	5 inches	40
Puritos	4¼ inches	29

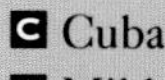

C Cuba
F Mild
Q Good-quality leaf and construction

Rafael Gonzalez

These are among the best of medium-priced Havanas, long well-known and appreciated by serious smokers. The box of this brand, originally created for the English market, carries the unusual legend: "These cigars have been manufactured from a secret blend of pure Vuelta Abajo tobaccos selected by the Marquez Rafael Gonzalez, Grandee of Spain. For more than 20 years this brand has existed. In order that the Connoisseur may fully appreciate the perfect fragrance they should be smoked either within one month of the date of shipment from Havana or should be carefully matured for about one year." The box used to carry a portrait of the great smoker Lord Lonsdale on the reverse side of the lid. The brand is made in the Romeo Y Julieta factory.

These first-class cigars have a delicate, but rich and subtle flavor, and complex aroma (they are much lighter, but have a hint of Montecristo to them). The label is very similar to Montecristo in both color and design. They are very well made and have good burning qualities. The Corona Extra is particularly reputed, as is the Lonsdale. The Cigarrito is a very good example of a size which is often unsatisfactory. The selection of sizes is commendably small. These are, in general, very classy cigars, among the mildest of Havanas.

SIZES

Name	Length: inches	Ring Gauge
Slenderella	7 inches	28
Lonsdale	6½ inches	42
Corona Extra	5⅝ inches	46
Petit Corona	5 inches	42
Petit Lonsdale	5 inches	42
Panetela Extra	5 inches	37
Panetela	4⅝ inches	34
Très Petit Lonsdale	4½ inches	40
Cigarrito	4½ inches	26
Demi Tasse	4 inches	30

TRES PETIT LONSDALE : LENGTH 4½ INCHES, RING GAUGE 40

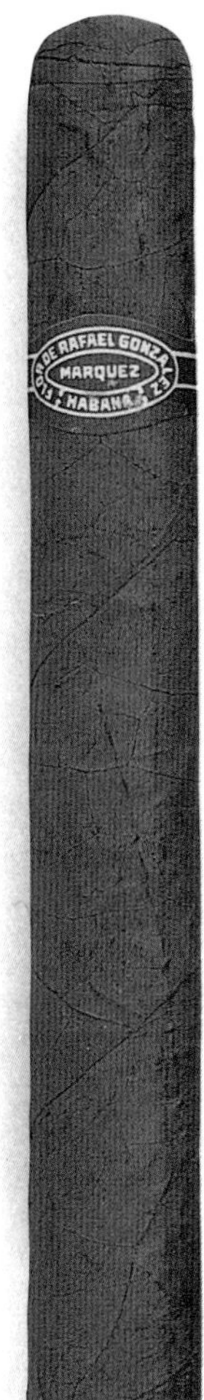

PETIT CORONA : LENGTH 5 INCHES, RING GAUGE 42

LONSDALE : LENGTH 6½ INCHES, RING GAUGE 42

- **C** Cuba
- **F** Mild
- **Q** The very best quality available

RAMON ALLONES

Dating from 1837, Ramon Allones, although not one of the best known of Havana names, is a favorite with many connoisseurs, among the best of the full-bodied cigars available. They are near the top of the list of medium-priced Cuban cigars – i.'e., below Cohiba and Montecristo, but up there with Upmann, Partagas, and Romeo Y Julieta. Most Ramon Allones are handmade, but there are a handful of machine-made sizes (Belvederes, Mille Fleurs, Delgados, and Toppers among them).

Ramon Allones are rolled in the Partagas factory (known for its full-bodied cigars) and have been since the factory was bought by the famous Cifuentes firm in the 1920s. The brand originated the 8–9–8 form of packaging.

The arms on the box are those of the Spanish royal house. Ramon Allones himself, emigrated from Galicia, in Spain, to Cuba, and was the first man to put colorful printed labels on his cigar boxes.

There is a good selection of Ramon Allones, all of them relatively full-bodied, and well made, with a strong aroma (similar to Partagas, but certainly less than Bolivar, also made in the same factory), good, dark wrappers, and excellent burning qualities. The smaller sizes tend to be lighter in color and somewhat milder. Rich in ligero leaf, these are not cigars for beginners. The 8–9–8 Corona is a good after-lunch choice, just as Gigantes (Prominente), 8–9–8 Churchill, or the Specially Selected (robusto) are all excellent choices after dinner. The very slim Ramonitas aren't recommended. These cigars age beautifully.

There are very good Dominican-produced Ramon Allones, with a similar band (but larger, and square, not round). They are very well made, mild to medium-bodied, and rather expensive. Most of the available sizes, unlike the Cuban brand, are named after letters of the alphabet. The Dominican brand, produced by General Cigar, have medium to dark Cameroon wrappers, Mexican binders, and fillers blended from Dominican, Jamaican, and Mexican tobacco. The Crystals are packed in individual glass tubes.

CUBAN SIZES

NAME	LENGTH: INCHES	RING GAUGE
Gigantes	7½ inches	49
8–9–8	6¹¹⁄₁₆ inches	43
Corona	5⅝ inches	42
Petit Corona	5 inches	42
Panetela	5 inches	35
Specially Selected	4¹³⁄₁₆ inches	50
Ramonitas	4¹³⁄₁₆ inches	26
Small Club Coronas	4⁵⁄₁₆ inches	42

DOMINICAN SIZES

NAME	LENGTH: INCHES	RING GAUGE
Redondos	7 inches	49
A	7 inches	45
Trumps	6¾ inches	43
Crystals	6¾ inches	43
B	6½ inches	42
D	5 inches	42

Small Club Coronas : Length $4\frac{5}{16}$ inches, Ring Gauge 42

Gigantes : Length $7\frac{1}{2}$ inches, Ring Gauge 49

Specially Selected : Length $4\frac{13}{16}$ inches, Ring Gauge 50

- **C** Cuba
- **F** Very full-bodied
- **Q** The very best quality available

- **C** Dominican Republic
- **F** Mild to medium
- **Q** Good-quality leaf and construction

RIATA

These Honduran cigars come in wrappers of moderate quality, are well made, burn and draw well, and have a pleasant if rather dull aroma and bouquet, and medium flavor. Binder, filler, and wrapper are all from Honduras.

SIZES

Name	Length: inches	Ring Gauge
No. 1000	8 inches	52
No. 900	7½ inches	50
No. 100	7 inches	30
No. 600	6⅞ inches	44
No. 200	6⅞ inches	35
No. 500	6⅝ inches	44
No. 800	6¼ inches	50
No. 300	6 inches	42
No. 400	5½ inches	44
No. 700	4¾ inches	50

C Honduras
F Mild to medium
Q Could be better

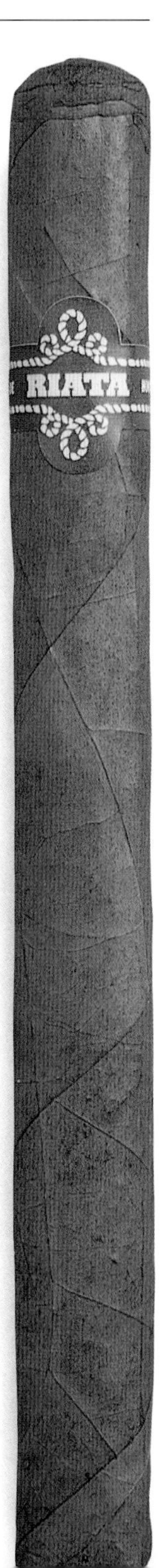

No. 900 : Length 7½ inches, Ring Gauge 50

ROMEO Y JULIETA

One of the very best-known Havana brands, particularly popular in Britain, Romeo Y Julieta cigars come in a huge choice of over 40 shapes and sizes. Many of them come in aluminum tubes, and there are also a large number of machine-made sizes. Despite the vast range, which inevitably means that not all sizes can be trusted, there are some very good cigars produced under this brand, many of them among the best available in their size.

The brand's early success was directly due to the efforts of Rodriguez Fernandez. "Pepin," as he was known, was originally manager of the Cabanas factory in Havana, but unhappy at its imminent takeover by American Tobacco, he resigned in 1903 to branch out on his own. Using his savings, he bought a little-known factory which, since 1875, had made cigars called Romeo Y Julieta solely for the Cuban domestic market. But he had bigger ideas, and encouraging his employees by distributing 30 percent of profits to heads of department, he traveled the world promoting the brand. Within two years, with his 1,400 workers, he had to move to a larger factory.

For monarchs, heads of state, and others, he specialized in providing personalized cigar bands (at one stage the factory was producing 20,000 different bands). Pepin remained devoted, almost obsessed by his brand, naming his racehorse Julieta, and trying to buy the House of Capulet in Verona, where Shakespeare's play was set. He couldn't quite do that, but was allowed to have a stand under the famous balcony, so that until 1939, every visitor was offered a free cigar in honor of the ill-starred lovers who gave the brand its name. He died in 1954.

The famous Romeo Y Julieta Churchills also come in tubes. They are very well-made cigars, with an excellent aroma, but the tubed versions can sometimes be rather fresh and, as a result, are

MADE IN HABANA, CUBA

not as well matured as the boxed versions. The Churchill sizes, with their distinctive gold bands (the others, apart from the Cedros series, are all red) are, nonetheless, classic medium to full-bodied cigars. The Corona size, often with colorado maduro wrappers, is very well-constructed but inconsistent in flavor. The Cedros de Luxe No. 1 (Lonsdale), is a dark, smooth, medium-bodied cigar, though sometimes not enough for lovers of this size. The Exhibicion No. 4 (Hermoso 4), with its oily wrapper, provides a rich smoke after a heavy meal and is a favorite with many connoisseurs. The Cedros de Luxe No. 2 is a very good corona, with plenty of personality. The Petit Julietas are among the best made and fullest-flavored in their size.

There is no meaningful difference between the various Churchill sizes, but some claim that the Prince of Wales is milder

CUBAN SIZES

NAME	LENGTH: INCHES	RING GAUGE
Churchill	7 inches	47
Prince of Wales	7 inches	47
Shakespeare	6⅞ inches	28
Cedros De Luxe No. 1	6½ inches	42
Corona Grande	6 inches	42
Belicosos	5½ inches	52
Exhibicion No. 3	5½ inches	43
Cedros De Luxe No. 2	5½ inches	42
Corona	5½ inches	42
Exhibicion No. 4	5 inches	48
Cedros De Luxe No. 3	5 inches	42
Petit Corona	5 inches	42
Très Petit Corona	4½ inches	40
Petit Julietas	4 inches	30

than the tubed version. Be sure not to confuse the tubed No. 1, No. 2, and No. 3 *De Luxe* with the similarly numbered tubes without the words "De Luxe" – which are machine-made, and much inferior. In Britain all tubed sizes are handmade, so you can smoke them without hesitation. The Cazadores (6⅜ inches, ring gauge 44), although handmade, is one of the cheapest cigars in the range for the good reason that it is made from less well-selected leaves. They are thus cigars of a different quality.

Dominican Republic cigars called Romeo Y Julietas are also produced in a vintage line wrapped in Connecticut shade and standard selections using darker Cameroon wrappers. Both types are very good and well made, the former offering a particularly delicate smoke. As with the Cuban Romeo Y Julietas, only a selection of sizes is given below.

SIZES

NAME	LENGTH: INCHES	RING GAUGE
Monarcas	8 inches	52
Churchills	7 inches	50
Presidentes	7 inches	43
Delgados	7 inches	32
Cetros	6½ inches	44
Romeos	6 inches	46
Palmas	6 inches	43
Brevas	5⅝ inches	38
Coronas	5½ inches	44
Panatelas	5¼ inches	35
Rothschilds	5 inches	50
Chiquitas	4¼ inches	32

C Dominican Republic
F Mild to medium
Q Superior quality

C Honduras
F Medium to full-bodied
Q Superior quality

VINTAGE SERIES

NAME	LENGTH: INCHES	RING GAUGE
Vintage V	7½ inches	50
Vintage IV	7 inches	48
Vintage II	6 inches	46
Vintage I	6 inches	43
Vintage III	4½ inches	50

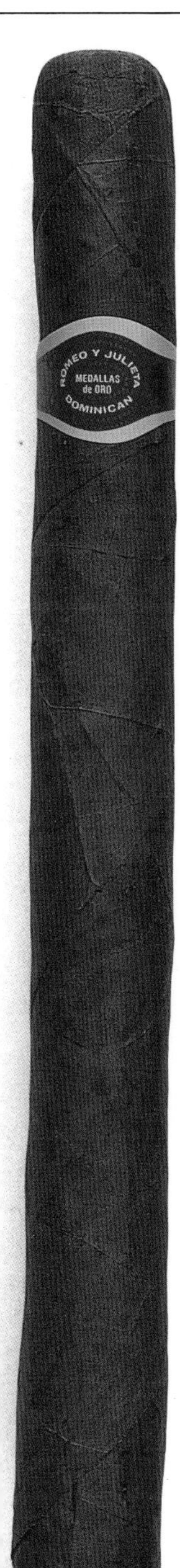

President : Length 7 inches, Ring Gauge 43

Monarcas : Length 8 inches, Ring Gauge 52

Churchill : Length 7 inches, Ring Gauge 50

CHURCHILL : LENGTH 7 INCHES, RING GAUGE 47

BELICOSOS : LENGTH 5½ INCHES, RING GAUGE 52

EXHIBICION NO. 4 : LENGTH 5 INCHES, RING GAUGE 48

C Cuba
F Mild to medium
Q The very best quality available

Royal Dominicana

These are mild to medium cigars made in the Dominican Republic with Mexican (Sumatra) wrappers and Dominican binders and fillers. They are well made and an easy smoke.

SIZES

Name	Length: inches	Ring Gauge
Churchill	7¼ inches	50
No. 1	6¾ inches	43
Corona	6 inches	46
Super Fino	6 inches	35
Nacional	5½ inches	43

C Dominican Republic
F Mild to medium
Q Good-quality leaf and construction

No. 1 : Length 6¾ inches, Ring Gauge 43

Corona : Length 6 inches, Ring Gauge 46

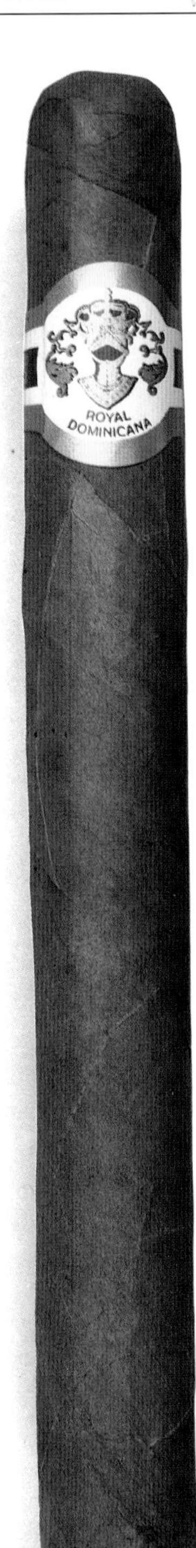

Churchill : Length $7\frac{1}{4}$ inches, Ring Gauge 50

Nacional : Length $5\frac{1}{2}$ inches, Ring Gauge 43

ROYAL JAMAICA

Formerly made in Jamaica, production of these cigars moved to the Dominican Republic following a hurricane in 1988 which destroyed both factories and tobacco crops. They remain among the best of mild cigars and come in a very wide choice of shapes and sizes – including the huge 64 ring gauge Goliath and the 10½-inch Ten Downing Street. Most Royal Jamaicas have Cameroon wrappers, but the fuller-bodied Maduro range uses wrappers from Brazil. They are all very well made.

SIZES

NAME	LENGTH: INCHES	RING GAUGE
Ten Downing Street	10½ inches	51
Goliath	9 inches	64
Churchill	8 inches	51
Giant Corona	7½ inches	49
Double Corona	7 inches	45
Doubloon	7 inches	30
Navarro	6¾ inches	34
Corona Grande	6½ inches	42
Tube No. 1	6½ inches	42
Park Lane	6 inches	47
Director 1	6 inches	45
Royal Corona	6 inches	40
New York Plaza	6 inches	40
Corona	5½ inches	40
Buccaneer	5½ inches	30
Petit Corona	5 inches	40
Churchill Minor	4½ inches	49
Pirate	4½ inches	30

MADURO RANGE

NAME	LENGTH: INCHES	RING GAUGE
Churchill	8 inches	51
Corona Grande	6½ inches	42
Corona	5½ inches	40
Buccaneer	5½ inches	30

TUBE NO. 1 : LENGTH $6\frac{1}{2}$ INCHES, RING GAUGE 42

PIRATE : LENGTH $4\frac{1}{2}$ INCHES, RING GAUGE 30

ROYAL CORONA : LENGTH 6 INCHES, RING GAUGE 40

C Dominican Republic
F Mild
Q Superior quality

Saint Luis Rey

This Havana brand was created some 50 years ago by British importers Michael de Keyser and Nathan Silverstone. The name originated after the success of the popular American film *The Bridge of San Luis Rey* (based on Thornton Wilder's play, and starring Akim Tamiroff and Alla Nazimova). By lucky chance, there was also a Cuban town called San Luis Obispo.

The characteristic cigars of the brand are heavyweight medium to strong cigars. They are made at the Romeo Y Julieta factory and are in many ways similar to Romeos. The brand has fans like Frank Sinatra (who likes the Lonsdale) and actor James Coburn. This is a very high-quality brand with a very limited production of only 60,000 cigars a year.

The cigars, which come in a predominantly white box and have a red label, are not to be confused with *San* Luis Rey, a brand made in Cuba for the German market. There is also a range of San Luis Reys machine-made in Germany for the mass market by Villiger using Havana leaf. San Luis Reys have a black label with a similar emblem.

These cigars are among the best Havanas available. The wrappers are dark to very dark, smooth and oily, and the flavor, although full-bodied, is very refined. The aroma of the best of these cigars is superb. The Regios (robusto) is a very fine smoke, as is the milder, and less full Churchill. Saint Luis Reys tend to be cheaper than most other Havanas (certainly others of comparable quality). The selection is small.

SIZES

Name	Length: inches	Ring Gauge
Churchill	7 inches	47
Lonsdale	6½ inches	42
Serie A	5⅝ inches	46
Corona	5⅝ inches	42
Regios	5 inches	48
Petit Corona	5 inches	42

CHURCHILL : LENGTH 7 INCHES, RING GAUGE 47

REGIOS : LENGTH 5 INCHES, RING GAUGE 48

CORONA : LENGTH $5\frac{5}{8}$ INCHES, RING GAUGE 42

C Cuba
F Very full-bodied
Q Superior quality

Sancho Panza

Sanchos : Length 9¼ inches, Ring Gauge 47

Not a well-known brand, but good, reliable Havanas, if a little too light and short on flavor for the real connoisseur. But for some, they offer a subtle, delicate, even elegant smoke, particularly the Molino (Lonsdale), although this cigar sometimes has a slightly salty taste which appeals to some smokers, not to others. Their construction sometimes leaves something to be desired: they don't burn as easily as they should. But the Corona Gigante is very well made. Even the torpedo-shaped Belicosos are mild (perhaps the mildest) for their type. The same applies to the Montecristo A-sized Sanchos. The line is small. These are good beginners' cigars, or for daytime smoking. The brand appears intermittently in Britain, but is very popular in Spain. There are plans to distribute it more widely.

SIZES

Name	Length: inches	Ring Gauge
Sanchos	9¼ inches	47
Corona Gigante	7 inches	47
Molino	6½ inches	42
Panetela Largo	6½ inches	28
Corona	5⅝ inches	42
Belicosos	5½ inches	52
Non Plus	5 1/16 inches	42
Bachilleres	4⅝ inches	40

C Cuba
F Mild
Q Superior quality

SANTA CLARA

Among the best of Mexican cigars. Made in San Andres with wrappers from the same area. The brand was founded in 1830, is medium flavored, and well made. There is a choice, in most sizes, of pale brown and dark wrappers.

SIZES

Name	Length: inches	Ring Gauge
No. I	7 inches	51
No. III	6⅝ inches	43
No. II	6½ inches	48
No. VIII	6½ inches	30
No. VI	6 inches	51
No. V	6 inches	44
No. VII	5½ inches	25
No. IV	5 inches	44
Quino	4¼ inches	30

C Mexico
F Mild to medium
Q Good-quality leaf and construction

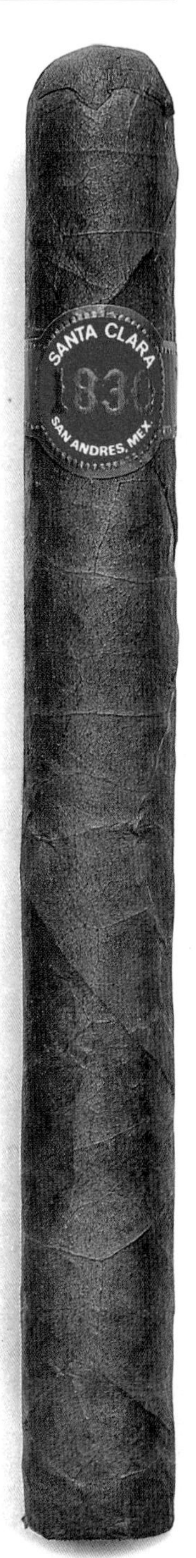

No. I : Length 7 inches, Ring Gauge 51

Santa Damiana

Santa Damiana was once a famous Cuban plantation and brand name. Now it is the name given to a relatively new brand of high-quality cigars, handmade in La Romana on the southeastern coast of the Dominican Republic.

The La Romana factory, near the luxurious Casa de Campo resort, is one of the most advanced handmade cigar factories in the world, applying modern quality-control techniques to the age-old skill of cigar rolling. Different blends and size names are used for the line sold in the United States as opposed to those available in Europe. The American sizes, named Seleccion No. 100, No. 300, and so on, contain a lighter blend of filler unlike the European line which, using traditional names, is designed to appeal to a preference for something fuller-flavored. Both are very well-made, consistent cigars.

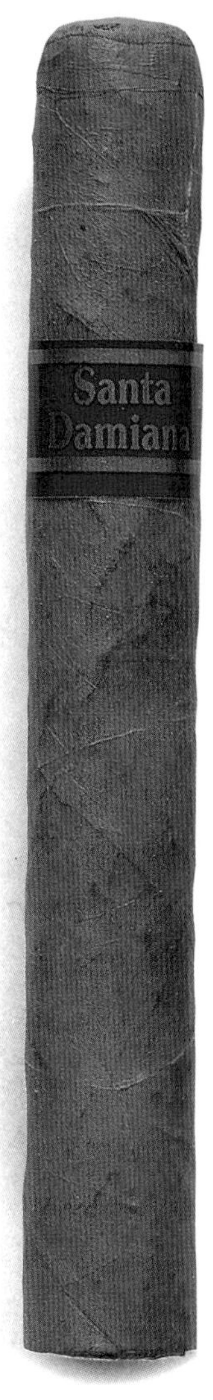

SELECCION 300 : LENGTH 5½ INCHES, RING GAUGE 46

SIZES

NAME	LENGTH: INCHES	RING GAUGE
Seleccion No. 800	7 inches	50
Seleccion No. 100 Churchill	6¾ inches	48
Seleccion No. 700	6½ inches	42
Seleccion No. 300	5½ inches	46
Corona	5½ inches	42
Seleccion No. 500	5 inches	50
Petit Corona	5 inches	42
Tubulares No. 400	5 inches	42
Panetela	4½ inches	36

C Dominican Republic
F Mild to medium
Q Superior quality

SOSA

This is a four-country blend cigar brand founded by Juan Sosa in the early 1970s and made in the Dominican Republic. Ecuadoran wrappers in darkish, natural, and maduro tones combine with Honduran binders and Brazilian and Dominican fillers to offer a pleasant and distinctive, medium to full flavor. There is a definite attempt here to go for the Cuban style of taste in a well-priced cigar.

CHURCHILL : LENGTH 7 INCHES, RING GAUGE 48

SIZES

NAME	LENGTH: INCHES	RING GAUGE
Magnum	7½ inches	52
Piramides #2	7 inches	64
Churchill	7 inches	48
Lonsdale	6½ inches	43
Governor	6 inches	50
Brevas	5½ inches	43
Wavell	4¾ inches	50

C Dominican Republic
F Medium to full
Q Could be better

SUERDIECK

One of the best-known Brazilian cigars, with a medium flavor. The line consists mostly of small ring-gauge sizes, a number of which are very similar. These are by no means connoisseurs' cigars – they are not particularly well made, and the mid-brown Brazilian wrappers (the cigars also use Brazilian fillers and binders) leave quite a lot to be desired. But some people like the flavor.

BRASILIA : LENGTH 5¼ INCHES, RING GAUGE 30

SIZES

NAME	LENGTH: INCHES	RING GAUGE
Fiesta	6 inches	30
Valencia	6 inches	30
Caballero	6 inches	30
Brasilia	5¼ inches	30
Mandarim Pai	5 inches	38

C Brazil
F Mild to medium
Q Could be better

TE-AMO

Made in Mexico, these cigars come in a wide range of sizes in both medium and mild versions for most of them. They are well made, but tend to be very tightly rolled, with little "give" which leads to problems of draw. The medium-flavored cigars come in a choice of light brown or maduro wrappers. The wrappers can be coarse and dry, without a noticeable bouquet aroma. These cigars, which have their fans, are distinctly different from Honduran and Dominican brands, but the flavor is less elegant, and they have a dull aroma. The brand once had quite a reputation for its flavor and aroma. It is no longer merited. But, as always with cigars, things might change again in the future.

SIZES

Name	Length: inches	Ring Gauge
C.E.O.	8½ inches	52
Churchill	7½ inches	50
Maximo	7 inches	54
Presidente	7 inches	50
Cabellero	7 inches	35
Picadore	7 inches	27
Contemplation	6⅞ inches	44
Relaxation	6⅝ inches	42
Torero	6½ inches	35
Toro	6 inches	50
Satisfaction	6 inches	46
Meditation	6 inches	42
Elegante	5½ inches	30
No. 4	5 inches	42
Epicure	5 inches	30
Torito	4½ inches	50

Presidente : Length 7 inches, Ring Gauge 50

C Mexico
F Mild to medium
Q Could be better

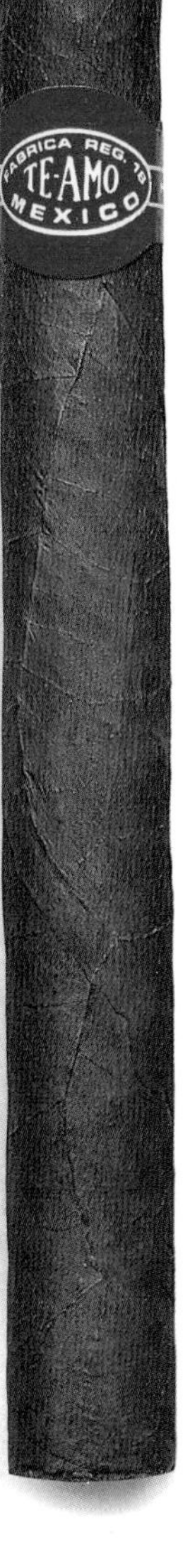

MEDITATION : LENGTH 6 INCHES, RING GAUGE 42

Temple Hall

This brand, founded in 1876, has been re-introduced by General Cigar. The Temple Hall estates are in Jamaica, and the cigars are a somewhat fuller-bodied version of Macanudo. Like Macanudo, the wrappers are Connecticut Shade and the filler blend a mixture of Jamaican, Dominican, and Mexican tobaccos. The binder is Mexican, from the San Andres area.

These are very well-made, subtle cigars, at or near the top of their line. Temple Hall make a special selection for Dunhill (slightly milder, with a different blend). The 450 is the only cigar which comes in a Mexican maduro wrapper. The brand consists of seven sizes.

SIZES

Name	Length: inches	Ring Gauge
700	7 inches	49
685	6⅞ inches	34
675	6¾ inches	45
625	6¼ inches	42
550	5½ inches	50
500	5 inches	31
450	4½ inches	49

450 : LENGTH 4½ INCHES, RING GAUGE 49

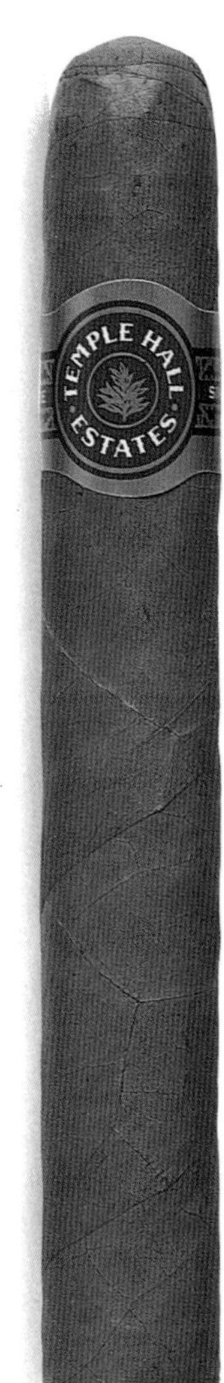

550 : LENGTH 5½ INCHES, RING GAUGE 50

700 : LENGTH 7 INCHES, RING GAUGE 49

C Jamaica
F Mild to medium
Q Superior quality

2¾

TRESADO

This is a relatively new Dominican brand, made and imported by the Consolidated Cigar Corporation. The cigars are well made and have a medium flavor.

SIZES

NAME	LENGTH: INCHES	RING GAUGE
No. 100	8½ inches	52
No. 200	7 inches	48
No. 400	6⅝ inches	44
No. 300	6 inches	46
No. 500	5½ inches	42

C Dominican Republic
F Mild to medium
Q Good-quality leaf and construction

NO. 200 : LENGTH 7 INCHES, RING GAUGE 48

TRINIDAD

This cigar is still not to be found in any store, but a few – a select few – people have had a chance to smoke it recently. They were the 164 guests at Marvin Shanken's Paris "Dinner of the Century" in October 1994. The one and only Trinidad size, a Laguito No. 1 like the Cohiba Lancero, was served as the first cigar. With a darker wrapper than you would find on any Cohiba and a rich, earthy flavor, there were those present who felt it might have been better suited to the end of the meal.

Mystery now shrouds the origin of this cigar. Non-smoking President Fidel Castro had been credited with its creation as an exclusive gift for heads of state to replace Cohiba after it went public. However, in his interview with *Cigar Aficionado* (summer 1994), Castro virtually denied any knowledge of its existence. He was happy to continue offering Cohibas to cigar enthusiasts of his acquaintance.

So, who's idea was it to ask the El Laguito factory to make Trinidad? As yet, outside official Cuban government circles, no one knows.

C Cuba
F Medium to full-bodied
Q The very best quality available

TRINIDAD : LENGTH 7½ INCHES, RING GAUGE 38

ZINO

Created by Zino Davidoff for the American market when his main brand was still made in Cuba, Zinos are well-tailored Honduran cigars which come in three brands. There is Mouton Cadet, appropriately clad in claret-colored bands and launched during a memorable mid-80s coast to coast tour by Zino himself accompanied by La Baronne Phillipine de Rothschild. These are medium-bodied cigars bearing interesting reddish-brown wrappers. There is the Connoisseur series of heavy-gauge cigars created for the opening of Davidoff's Madison Avenue store, and the standard line, with gold bands, including the 7-inch, 50 gauge Veritas, which gives rise to one of advertising's few classical Latin puns – In Zino Veritas.

SIZES

Name	Length: inches	Ring Gauge
Connoisseur 100	7¾ inches	50
Connoisseur 200	7½ inches	46
Veritas	7 inches	50
Zino Tubos No. 1	6¾ inches	34
Elegance	6¾ inches	34
Junior	6½ inches	30
Tradition	6¼ inches	44
Connoisseur 300	5¾ inches	46
Diamond	5½ inches	40
Princesse	4½ inches	20

MOUTON-CADET SERIES

Name	Length: inches	Ring Gauge
No. 1	6½ inches	44
No. 2	6 inches	35
No. 3	5¾ inches	36
No. 4	5⅛ inches	30
No. 5	5 inches	44
No. 6	5 inches	50

VERITAS : LENGTH 7 INCHES, RING GAUGE 50

CONNOISSEUR 100 : LENGTH 7¾ INCHES, RING GAUGE 50

MOUTON CADET NO. 6 : LENGTH 5 INCHES, RING GAUGE 50

C Honduras
F Mild to medium
Q Superior quality

THE STRENGTH OF CIGARS

Cuba is unique to the extent that all Havanas or Habanos are blended from tobaccos grown on the island. They tend to offer medium to full flavors but the enormous variety of leaves available can produce surprisingly mild smokes in certain brands.

Cigars from other places like the Dominican Republic and Honduras are usually made from tobaccos taken from several countries. Hard and fast rules on flavors are therefore impossible to lay down. As a rough guide: Connecticut shade wrapped cigars with Dominican fillers tend towards mildness; maduro wrappers bring a sweetness to the taste, and in general Honduran and Nicaraguan fillers add spiciness.

Below is a selection of cigars by strength of flavor:

Country of Origin

C Cuba
CI Canary Islands
D Dominican Republic
H Honduras
J Jamaica
M Mexico
N Nicaragua

Mild

Ashton **D**
Casa Blanca **D**
Cuesta-Rey **D**
Macanudo **J**
Pleiades **D**
Rafael Gonzalez **C**
Royal Jamaica **D**
H. Upmann **C**

Mild to Medium

Arturo Fuente **D**
Avo **D**
Bauza **D**
Canaria D'Oro **D**
Davidoff **D**
Don Diego **D**
Griffin's **D**
La Invicta **H**
Joya de Nicaragua **N**
Primo del Rey **D**
Punch **C**
Rey del Mundo **C**
Romeo Y Julieta **C**
Santa Damiana **D**
Te-Amo **M**
Temple Hall **J**

Medium to Full

Aliados **H**
Cohiba **C**
V Centennial **H**
Don Ramos **H**
Dunhill **D**
Excalibur **H**
Henry Clay **D**
Mocha **H**
Montecristo **C**
Montecruz **D**
Por Larranaga **C**
Paul Garmirian **D**

Full

Bolivar **C**
Partagas **C**
Ramon Allones **C**
Saint Luis Rey **C**

3
BUYING AND STORING CIGARS

When you buy a box of handmade cigars (certainly Havanas) you should ask to open the box to check the contents. No decent cigar merchant should refuse. If he does, he either doesn't know his business, or there is probably something wrong with the cigars. The first judgment to make is purely visual: they have to look good. Make sure that the cigars are all of the same color. They should be properly matched: darkest on the left, lightest on the right. If there is any significant variation in color, it would be sensible to reject the cigars, as they are likely to be inconsistent in flavor, and the box might possibly have escaped final quality control in the factory. If the cigars differ significantly in color and the box is already open, it is more likely to mean that some of the cigars have come from another box (or somebody: customs, the cigar merchant, has been messing around with them) – another good reason for rejecting them. The spiral of the wrapper leaf should be in the same direction on all the cigars. Don't be afraid to smell the cigars to see if you find the bouquet agreeable – it is part of what you are paying for. If they smell good, they should taste good, too. Smell the cut ends, or take one cigar out, and smell the gap where it lay: that way you will experience the bouquet at its fullest.

And feel one or two of the cigars. They should give slightly when you press gently between finger and thumb, but spring back to shape. They should feel smooth. If they make a noise, they are too old or dry. If they don't regain their shape, they are not well

THE DAVIDOFF SHOP, JERMYN STREET, LONDON.

PREVIOUS PAGE: GEORGETOWN TOBACCO, WASHINGTON D.C. OWNER DAVID BERKEBILE.

made. If the cigar shows no resilience when you press or is mushy, it has been badly stored and will smoke badly. A fresh cigar (less than three months old) will spring back to shape even if your finger and thumb make the two sides almost touch.

If possible, buy cigars in large quantities (boxes of 10 or 25, say) rather than cartons of five which are often less good and less consistent than larger quantities. Nor is it as easy to inspect a cellophaned carton as it is simply to open a cigar box. Some large cigar stores sell cigars in their own boxes or with their "own label." This is normally a marketing ploy: if you have an empty box or two at home, buy them loose; otherwise, you are simply paying for the fancy packaging. The same applies to cigars in polished boxes: if you have the option, buy them in regular cedar, unless you are very fond of boxes or want to present the cigars as a gift. Unless you have sophisticated storage facilities, buy only what you can smoke in the near future (a month or two, say).

Cigars in aluminum tubes lined with cedar (invented by H. Upmann), though very convenient to carry, can sometimes be rather dry as the tubes are not completely airtight. They occasionally lose their bouquet and tend not to be as well matured as cigars in boxes. This applies particularly to small sizes, whatever the manufacturer may claim on the tube. You can, on the other hand, find perfectly well-conditioned cigars in tubes. In the case of the famous Romeo Y Julieta Churchill, the tube states: "The rich aromatic flavor of this fine Havana cigar will be protected by the aluminum container until opened." But many would disagree.

Cigars wrapped in cellophane can be just as good as those left loose in the box (except, that is, if they are machine-made). They keep well, but mature less. Sometimes cellophane turns brown by absorbing the oils from the cigar it contains. This shouldn't make a difference to the quality of the cigar, particularly if it is then properly humidified. Handmade Havanas rarely come in cellophane, although some sizes of Cohiba do, when sold in small packs.

Some cigars, the Havana H. Upmann Cristales (a corona size), for instance, come in hermetically sealed jars. These are meant to be "fresh" cigars, theoretically unmatured, and tasting like the cigar would shortly after it was actually made.

London (with shops like the 200-year-old Fox & Lewis, Davidoff, and Dunhill) is acknowledged to be the best place in Europe to buy handmade cigars, certainly Havanas. The London branch of Davidoff sells some 400,000 handmade cigars a year in 220 different sizes and brands. But British import and tobacco taxes

The Davidoff shop, New York.

THE HISTORIC DUNHILL SHOP, LONDON.

are high, and the cigars don't come cheap. Paris and Geneva (the headquarters of Davidoff) are also good places to buy. You are unlikely to find non-Cuban cigars using Cuban brand names in most of the leading European cigar shops, so there should be little confusion. Although Spain imports more cigars than anywhere else in Europe (the Spaniards smoke around 30 million Havanas a year, compared to 5 million in Britain), the quality of Havanas there, with many machine-mades on the market to boot, is often dubious, though prices are cheaper than in most of the rest of Europe. Smoking cigars is a particular custom at bullfights. There is a good selection of non-Cuban handmades to be found in London and, of course, in the major cigar stores in the United States.

Beware of apparent bargains – in sales, for instance. These are sometimes machine-made cigars bearing famous Havana labels. As always, check the box carefully. The same applies at airports, where duty-free prices can look very attractive. Storage conditions are often poor, but fast turnover can mean the cigars are smokable. Inspection is not permitted, so there's a risk. You should certainly steer clear of small tobacco stores, news stands, and the like: the cigars will almost certainly be old and badly stored.

Cigars, like any natural product, need to be carefully kept. They should be protected from extremes of temperature and kept in a humidified environment – ideally at 60°–70°F with 65–70 percent humidity. This may be difficult to achieve, particularly in air-conditioned or centrally heated homes. But at the very least, you should keep your cigars in an airtight cupboard or box, away from any heat source, in preferably the coolest place in the house. Keep the cigars in their cedar boxes – the cedar helps to preserve them. You could put a damp sponge in the cupboard. Put the cigar boxes in plastic bags if you like, to stop evaporation, spraying a little water into the bag before you put the box in. If you put a damp sponge or a glass of water in the bag, not too close to the cigars, it will help humidify them (as long as the bag isn't completely sealed – so that there is some air flow – and the box of cigars is partially open).

Some experts suggest that you store cigars in an airtight bag in the vegetable crisper compartment of your refrigerator, but in that case you should take a cigar out of the fridge at least half an hour before you want to smoke it, so that it can get back to room temperature. This is a method of storage which has many detractors, and one you have to be particularly careful with. If you put cigars in the refrigerator, the airtight bag (with excess air expelled before you close or seal it) is essential. You can also get small humidifiers from leading cigar merchants. These come in different shapes and sizes (ranging from pill box types to small strips of plastic), and you put them in the cigar box (having removed a cigar or two). The moistened sponge or chalk in these devices will help keep the cigars humidified, (but be careful to check once a month that the sponge hasn't dried out). Metal tubes, which work in a similar way, are also available.

Many importers and merchants use Zip Lock or other sealable heavy plastic bags to send cigars to major clients, and they are very useful, particularly if you are traveling with cigars. Keep them in the box, and put a slightly damp sponge in the bag or spray the inside of the bag with a little water.

If cigars are stored in a warm climate, bugs can sometimes appear – the tobacco beetle, in particular. Heat allows the larvae to hatch. You should never store cigars anywhere near direct sunlight, or exposed to sea breezes. If you store cigars at a low temperature, you have to raise the humidity to compensate.

Humidors come normally made of wood such as walnut, mahogany, and rosewood (though there are also plexiglass models on the market), usually at fancy prices, and in many sizes. They are only really worth buying if you smoke cigars regularly. You should make sure that the lid, which should be heavy, closes tightly and that there is a hygrometer to monitor the humidity level. The humidor should be well made and unvarnished inside. Keep an eye on it, and remember, the humidor only looks after humidity, not the temperature, so you still have to find a suitable location for it. It's useful if the humidor comes with trays at various levels, so that you can store different sizes separately and rotate cigars within the box. Prices can range from $200 to over $2,000 – but at the top end you are paying for the humidor as furniture as much as for its functional use. For example, Viscount Linley, cabinet-maker and nephew of Britain's Queen Elizabeth, now offers beautifully crafted humidors through Dunhill starting at $2,000. The plexi-glass models retail for under $200 and are serviceable enough. Choose your humidor carefully: many are ineffective or need careful monitoring.

Small humidors made of wood or leather are also available for travelers. Some firms such as Davidoff even market briefcases with special cigar and accessory compartments, or built-in mini-humidors. There are number of pocket cigar cases on the market. The best are made of leather, and the most convenient design is the expandable, rigid "telescope" type which can take large or small cigars. Some pocket cases come with mini-moisturizing units. For the cigar smoker who has everything, there are any number of items on the market such as brass, silver, and gold-plated cigar tubes, fancy lighters, and silver match holders.

HUMIDORS. THE SELECTION IS HUGE.

If cigars are very dry, they will be difficult to revive satisfactorily. But, essentially, if moisture can escape from a cigar, it can also be replaced. One of the simplest methods, which usually works, is to put the open box of cigars in a large plastic bag, which is partially, but not completely, closed (it is essential to have a little air flow). You should also put a glass of water or a moist sponge in the bag. Rotate the cigars every few days, remembering also to bring cigars from the bottom of the box to the top, and within three weeks or so the cigars should return to smokable condition. It is very much a matter of trial and error, and means that you have to keep a careful eye on things. They will, however, having been dry in the first place, have lost much of their bouquet and won't compare to a well-kept cigar. In any event, cigars lose moisture slowly and need to regain it equally slowly. You need patience: attempting drastic measures will only ruin the cigars for good.

Another simple way of reviving a box of cigars, after traveling for instance, is to turn it upside-down, and put it under a gently running faucet. Be careful: the bottom of the box should be moistened by the water, but no more. You could use a sponge as an alternative method of dampening the bottom of the box. Shake off excess water and put the box in an airtight bag. The cigars should be in good shape after a couple of days.

Some major cigar stores, particularly if you are a regular customer, will revive a box of cigars for you in their humidified room (it takes around a month) as a favor. The charming and knowledgeable Edward Sahakian of the Davidoff shop in London will even provide this service for people who aren't regular customers – at no cost. "The pleasure of doing it is sufficient for both him and myself," he says.

Top cigar stores will also store cigars for regular clients.

PLACING THE CIGARS IN A PARTIALLY CLOSED POLYTHENE BAG IS ONE WAY OF REPLACING LOST MOISTURE.

The only serious collectors' market in cigars is in prerevolutionary Havanas. They demand premium prices, about 5 or 6 times higher than the current retail price. The best place to find them is in London, because of the old tradition of laying down large cigar reserves at the main cigar shops. These cigars usually come onto the market when someone realizes that he will never get through the reserve, or when he dies (sometimes there is no obvious beneficiary). They are particularly attractive to American smokers, who have been able to buy and import them with a clear conscience since the trade embargo was imposed on Cuba in 1962. Unopened boxes are the most sought-after, as are sizes and brands which have now disappeared.

You can tell a prerevolutionary box because, the underside will read: "Made in Havana, Cuba," as opposed to the use of Spanish after the revolution.

Whether such old cigars are actually worth buying is a different question. As with old wine vintages, it is a matter of luck. If they have been properly stored and date no earlier than the 1950s, they might well still provide very satisfactory and interesting smokes. But, however well stored, they could just as easily be mere shadows of their former selves, musty with little bouquet. Dark cigars (colorado, colorado maduro, or maduro) are the best bets. Cigars really shouldn't be kept, even in the best storage conditions, for more than 10 to 15 years: the longer you leave cigars, the more of their bouquet and aroma they will lose.

THE MARK ON ANY PREREVOLUTIONARY BOX OF CIGARS.

Cigar Merchants' Directory

Australia

MELBOURNE
Benjamins Fine Tobacco
Shop 16,
Myer House Arcade,
250 Elizabeth Street
Tel: 3 663 2879

Daniels Fine Tobaccos
Melbourne Central,
300 Lonsdale Street
Tel: 3 663 6842

SYDNEY
Alfred Dunhill
74 Castlereagh Street
Tel: 2 231 5511

Cigar Divan at Pierpoints,
Hotel Intercontinental
17 Macquarie St
Tel: 2 230 0200

TOORAK, VICTORIA
J&D of Alexanders
Shop 7, Tok H Centre
459, Toorak Road
Tel: 3 827 1477

Canada

CALGARY
Cavendish-Moore's
Tobacco Ltd
Penny Lane Market
Tel: 403 269 2716

MONTREAL
Blatter & Blatter
365, President Kennedy
Tel: 514 845 2028

TORONTO
Thomas Hinds Tobacconist
8, Cumberland Street
Tel: 416 927 7703

Havana House
87, Avenue Road
Tel: 416 927 9070

VICTORIA
Old Morris Tobacconist
1116, Government Street
Tel: 604 382 4811

WINDSOR
Thomas Hinds Tobacconist
473 Ouelette Avenue
Tel: 519 254 0017

WINNIPEG
Havana House
185, Carlton Street
Tel: 204 942 0203

VANCOUVER
R. J. Clarke Tobacconist
No 3, Alexander Street
Tel: 604 687 4136

France

PARIS
A Casa del Habano
69 Boulevard Saint-Germain
Tel: 1 4549 2430

La Civette
157 rue Saint Honore
Tel: 42 61 61 07

Les Quatre-Temps
La Defense,
Centre Commercial des
Quatre-Temps
Tel: 47 74 75 28

La Tabagie
10 rue du Depart
Tel: 45 38 65 18

Germany

BERLIN
Horst Kiwus
Kantstr. 56
Tel: 30 3124450

Ka De We
Tauentzienstr. 21–24
Tel: 030-21210

HAMBURG
Duske u. Duske
Großen Bleichen 36
Tel: 040-343385

Pfeifen Timm
Jungfernstieg 26
Tel: 040-345187

KÖLN
Pfeifenhaus Heinrichs
Hahnenstr. 2
Tel: 0221-256483

MUNICH
Max Zechbauer
Residenzstrasse 10
Tel: 49 89 29 68 86

Hong Kong

The Cohiba Cigar Divan
The Lobby,
The Mandarin Hotel

The Netherlands

AMSTERDAM
Hajenius
92-96 Rokin
Tel: 31 20 23 74 94

Spain

BARCELONA
Gimeno
101 Paseo de Gracia
Tel: 34 3 217 92 71

MADRID
Gonzales de Linares
Paseo Habana No. 26
Tel: 34 1 262 22 82

SANTIAGO
Calle Alcala No 18
Tel: 34 1 221 47 16

Switzerland

GENEVA
Davidoff & Cie
2 Rue de Rive
Tel: 41 223 10 90 49 1211

Gerard Pere et Fils
Hotel Noga Hilton
19 Quai du Mont Blanc
Tel: 41 227 32 65 11

ZURICH
Durr
Bahnhofplatz 6
Tel: 41 12 11 63 23

UNITED KINGDOM

BATH
Frederick Tranter
5, Church Street
Abbey Green
Tel: 01225 466197

BIRMINGHAM
John Hollingsworth & Son
5, Temple Row
Tel: 0121 236 7768

CAMBRIDGE
Harrison & Simmonds
17, St. Johns Street
Tel: 01223 324515

EDINBURGH
Herbert Love
31, Queensferry Street
Tel: 0131 225 8082

GLASGOW
The Tobacco House
9, St. Vincent's Place
Tel: 0141 226 4586

LEEDS
Astons
17, Thornton Arcade
Tel: 0113 234 7435

LONDON
Davidoff of London
35, St. James's Street, SW1.
Tel: 0171 930 3079

Alfred Dunhill Limited
30, Duke Street,
St. James's, SW1.
Tel: 0171 499 9566

Fox/Lewis Cigar Merchants
19, St. James's Street, SW1.
Tel: 0171 930 3787

Harrods
Knightsbridge, SW1.
Tel: 0171 730 1234

Havana Club
165 Sloane St, SW1
Tel: 0171-245 0890

Sautter of Mayfair
106, Mount Street, W1.
Tel: 0171 499 4866

Selfridges
Oxford Street, W1.
Tel: 0171 629 1234

Shervingtons
337, High Holborn, WC1.
Tel: 0171 405 2929

W. Thurgood
London Wall, EC2M 5QD.
Tel: 0171 628 5437

G. Ward
60, Gresham Street, EC2.
Tel: 0171 606 4318

MANCHESTER
Astons
Royal Exchange Centre
Tel: 0161 832 7895

STRATFORD-UPON-AVON
Lands
29, Central Chambers,
Henley Street
Tel: 01789 292508

UNITED STATES

CHICAGO
Jack Schwartz Importers
175 W. Jackson
Tel: 312-782 7898

KANSAS CITY
Diebels Sportsmens Gallery
426, Ward Parkway
Tel: 800 305 2988

MIAMI BEACH
Mike's Cigars
465 Arthur Godfrey Road
Tel: 305-538 6707

NEW HAVEN
The Owl Shop
268, College Street
CT 06510

NEW YORK, NY
Arnold's Cigar Store
323 Madison Avenue
Tel: 212-697 1477

Davidoff of Geneva
535 Madison Avenue
54th Street
Tel: 212 751 9060

De La Concha Tobacconists
1390 Avenue of the Americas
Tel: 212 757 3167

Nat Sherman Inc.
500 Fifth Avenue
Tel: 212 246 5500

PHILADELPHIA
Holt Cigar Co. Inc.
1522 Walnut Street
Tel: 800 523 1641

PORTLAND
Rich Cigar Store Inc.
801 Southwest Alder Street
Tel: 800 669 1527

SAN ANTONIO
The Humidor Inc.
6900 San Pedro Avenue*111
TX 78216

SANTA MONICA
Tinder Box-Santa Monica
2729 Wilshire Blvd.
Tel: 213 828 2313

SANTA ROSA
The Pipe Squire
346 Coddington Center

SELMA
J. R. Tobacco of America Inc.
I-95 at Route 70
Tel: 800 572 4427

WASHINGTON
Georgetown Tobacco
3144 M North West
Washington DC
Tel: 202 338 5100

INDEX

binder leaves 27
Bock, Gustave 44
Brazilian cigars 203

Canary Isles cigars 17, 102–4, 152
capping a cigar 30
Castro, Fidel 14, 78, 209
Chateau de la Fuente 58, 61
Cienfuegos, Cuba 181
Cifuentes family 14, 69
cigar
  bands 44
  boxes 40–3
  cases 219
  production 20–40
  sizes 45–7
  structure 27–8
  aging 48–9
  buying 214–17
  history of 9–14
  lighting 51–2
  selecting 47–9
  smoking 51–3
  storing 218–19
  strength of 212
Cigar Aficonado, Magazine 6, 15, 58, 209
Connecticut, tobacco growing in 10, 17
Cuba
  history of cigar production in 10–11, 13–16
  production methods in 31–8
  tobacco growing areas 18–19
  see also Havana cigars
Cubatabaco 14–16, 42, 86, 149
curing & fermenting 22–6
cutters 51

Davidoff, Zino 86, 113, 210
Davidoff
  shops 215–17
Dominican Republic
  brands 58–65, 68–75, 84–9, 92–3, 102–4, 110, 113–19, 126–8, 131, 134, 140, 144, 154–76, 186, 190, 193–6, 201–2, 208
  cigar production in 14–15, 17, 28, 38
dried cigars, reviving 220
Dunhill, Alfred 102

El Laguito factory 31, 78–9, 148

factory codes 43
Fuente, Arturo 58–9

Garcia family 148
Gener, José 120–1
Gonzales, José Manuel 148
Guevara, Che 78

H. Upmann factory 31, 40–1, 114, 148
handmade cigars 28–38
  compared with machine-made 38–40
Havana cigars
  brands 70, 78–82, 86–91, 105–6, 110–12, 114–16, 120–2, 133, 135–6, 148–151, 162–4, 171–2, 177–186, 188–192, 198–9, 209
  history of 13–16
  production methods 31–8
Honduran cigars 56–7, 66–7, 76–7, 94–101, 106–9, 120–7, 139, 147, 177–180, 187 210–211
humidifiers 218
humidors 219

J.R. Cigars 124–9
Jamaican cigars 141–3, 206–7

La Corona factory 31, 134, 177
Laguito, *see* El Laguito
Lara, Avelino 78
ligero leaves 27
Lopez, Manuel 177

machine-made cigars 38–40
Martí, José 14
Menendez family 14, 141, 148, 152, 162
Mexican cigars 145, 200, 204–5

Newman family 84–5
Nicaraguan cigars 129–30

Palicio family 14–15
Partagas 31–2
Partido, Cuba 19
Philippine cigars 38, 69–71, 110–11
Pinar del Rio, Cuba 18–19
Putnam, Israel 10

Raleigh, Sir Walter 10
Ribera, Eduardo 78–9
Rodriguez Fernandez, "Pepin" 188
rolling 28–30
  of Havana cigars 33–6
Romeo Y Julieta factory 31, 105, 197
Rothman, Lew 124–7

San Juan Y Martinez, Cuba 18–19, 120
San Luis, Cuba 18–19
seco leaves 27
Sosa, Juan 202–3

Tamayo, Emilia 78
Tampa, Florida 84
tobacco
  plant 20
  plantations, early 10
  production 20–6

volado leaves 28
Vuelta Abajo, Cuba 18–19, 78

wrapper leaves 20–1, 22, 24–5, 26, 27